101 REASONS TO LOVE PRO WRESTLING

BY
MIKEY MIGO

Copyright © 2023 Digital Lizard Productions
All rights reserved.
ISBN: 9798375337791

DEDICATION

To the Maniaks.

INTRODUCTION

From year to year, month to month, week to week, and day to day people across the world are obsessed with the phenomenon that is professional wrestling.

But why?

There are many components of professional wrestling that should be both understood and celebrated.

In no particular order...

1. SUSPENSION OF DISBELIEF 9
2. THE STEEL CHAIR 11
3. HISTORY 13
4. LAST MINUTE KICK OUTS 19
5. THE LINGO 21
6. DAVID VS. GOLIATH 24
7. SHIRTS 26
8. DRAMA 28
9. PRO ATHLETE CROSSOVERS 30
10. CHAMPIONSHIP BELTS 33
11. DEBUTS WITH VIGNETTES 35
12. TOURNAMENTS 38
13. DIVERSITY 40
14. ENTRANCE MUSIC 43
15. CHEAP POP 46
16. HARDCORE 48
17. EVERYDAY IS HALLOWEEN 51
18. THE HOT TAG 53
19. ROBES 55
20. HIGH SPOTS 57
21. INSIDE POLITICS 59
22. FAMILY TRADITION 62
23. DREAM MATCHES 64
24. MUSIC GIMMICKS 67
25. STABLES 69
26. TABLE SPOTS 72
27. THE LOOK AROUND HANDSHAKE 74
28. HYPOTHETICAL ENTRANCE MUSIC 76

29. LADDER MATCHES	78
30. HEEL TURNS	82
31. FIGHTING ALL OVER	85
32. THE VIDEO GAMES	87
33. CRYING CHILDREN	92
34. CROWD CHANTS	94
35. GIMMICK MATCHES	97
36. DISCOVERING NEW TALENT	100
37. GRAND ENTRANCES	102
38. TASSELS	104
39. TRYING IT AT HOME	106
40. THE SPANISH ANNOUNCE TABLE	108
41. THE REF BUMP	110
42. FANTASY BOOKING	112
43. SURPRISE PINS	114
44. THE EXPOSED TURNBUCKLE	116
45. REINVENTED CHARACTERS	118
46. SUPER CARDS	121
47. AUTO DESTRUCTION	123
48. CREATURE FEATURES	125
49. MANAGERS	127
50. HOUSE SHOWS	129
51. KAYFABE	131
52. PILLMANIZING	134
53. CONSISTENT PROGRAMING	137
54. CREATING NEW FANS	139
55. CONVENTIONS	141
56. HOLLYWOOD INTERPRETATIONS	143
57. SNEAK ATTACKS	145
58. BLOOD	147
59. MAGAZINES	150
60. BIG LEAPS	152
61. BITTER RIVALS	154
62. INDEPENDENTS	156
63. SUBMISSION HOLDS	159
64. RING BELL SPOTS	161
65. KENDO STICKS	163
66. FINISHING MOVES	166
67. SHOOT INTERVIEWS	168
68. CHEAP HEAT	171

69. HATS	173
70. GIANTS	175
71. PSYCHOLOGY	177
72. ROMANCE	179
73. ACTION FIGURES	182
74. CAGE MATCHES	188
75. BATTLE ROYALS	192
76. AUTHORITY FIGURES	196
77. OBVIOUS DISTRACTIONS	200
78. MASKS	202
79. GREAT PROMOS	205
80. INVASION ANGLES	208
81. MYSTERY OPPONENTS & PARTNERS	210
82. LOSER LEAVES TOWN	213
83. INJURY COMEBACKS	216
84. THE TAG ROPE	218
85. LOGOS	220
86. PUNCHING THE AIR IN DESPERATION	222
87. TAUNTS	224
88. FACE TURNS	226
89. PATRIOTISM	229
90. POST-MATCH RESPECT	232
91. MISTING, POWDER, AND FIRE!	234
92. ROYALTY	237
93. REBELLION	239
94. IRON MAN MATCHES	241
95. SIGNS IN THE CROWD	244
96. PODCASTS	246
97. POP CULTURE POP-UPS	248
98. POSTERS	252
99. SACRIFICE	254
100. COMEDY	256
101. ANYTHING… CAN… HAPPEN	259

101 REASONS TO LOVE PRO WRESTLING

1. SUSPENSION OF DISBELIEF

The willingness to suspend one's critical faculties and believe something surreal.

It's a sacrifice of realism and logic in favor of enjoyment.

The term was first introduced by the poet Samuel Taylor Coleridge way back in 1817.

The term itself is only about two hundred years old, but the idea of having an audience "play along" goes back decades, centuries, and even millenniums.

In theatre and writing, it is the act of engaging the audience's willingness to overlook reality and enjoy the premise in the world it is presented in.

But what about professional wrestling?

What disbeliefs are we being asked to suspend?

Are we supposed to believe that two grown adults are so mad at each other that they want to settle their differences in an elevated square surrounded by three ropes?

In front of a sports arena filled of screaming spectators?

While thousands, or even millions, watch at home on a weekly basis?

All of this while wearing colorful outfits and pursuing the right to wear a gold and jewel encrusted belt and be champion?

And we're just supposed to accept that if we, the fan, cheer loud enough our favorites will gain energy to overcome?

Are we supposed to believe that some of these wrestlers are actually the walking dead, monsters, warriors, beasts, barbers, repo men, witch doctors, clowns, cowboys, vampires, and just about any other character that could be imagined.

And then we're supposed to actually believe that this is a family business?

We're supposed to just accept that someone can attack their boss and not lose their job and livelihood?

We're supposed to believe giants can be defeated?

We're supposed to believe that this spectacle is responsible for some of Hollywood's biggest stars?

We're supposed to believe that boyhood dreams can come true?

We're supposed to believe tomorrow is another day?

We're supposed to believe that legends live forever?

If you want to be a fan of professional wrestling, then your answer to all of these questions should be "Oh Hell Yeah!"

Before attendance numbers, ticket sales, buy rates, ratings and merch sales suspension of disbelief is the currency that professional wrestling is measured on.

If we believe, if we are engaged, if we are lost in the world that is created, then ultimately, they are doing their jobs.

And when they do their job properly, professional wrestling is a work of athletic art. It's the same magic that gets both an eager child and a grown adult on their feet cheering, jeering, and anticipating the reveal of the next trick.

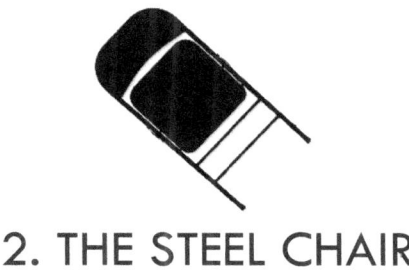

2. THE STEEL CHAIR

The steel chair is an off shoot of a folding chair, a light portable piece of seating furniture.

The folding chair's roots go back to 15th century BC. Yes, that's BC. The folding chair itself was patented by John Cham in 1855, but it would be 1947 when the great Fredric Arnold created the first ever aluminum folding chair.

Ten years later, Mr. Arnold's Brooklyn, New York company was making close to 15,000 chairs a day.

Meanwhile, pro wrestling shows were often held in auditoriums, convention centers, and venues that would have bleachers and chairs for the spectators to sit in.

So, it would have only been natural for a Street Fight, Death Match, or No Holds Barred Match to spill into the seats.

Brawlers like the Funk brothers, who were also outstanding grapplers in their own right, took it upon themselves to take the fans seats back since their fans were often only using the edge of them anyway.

By the early 80's all of the wrestling territories were embracing the idea of bloody brawls. None that would have been complete without a chair or two.

The use of this foreign object has often been reserved for the most hated of rivals and in the most desperate of situations.

The 1990's saw a surge in steel chair violence.

Wrapped in barbed wire, lit on fire, or used in tandem the steel chair's place in history cannot be ignored.

Everyone was swinging chairs.

Everyone was taking heads off.

Everyone was crushing skulls.

Really, everyone.

Okay, maybe one guy didn't...

Oh, nope. He did too.

Times have changed since these brutal acts of interior design. Thanks to advancements in science and medicine it is now frowned upon to swing a chair at someone's skull. Concussions are real. This doesn't mean it doesn't happen, but when it does it's met with controversy.

This doesn't mean that the steel chair's best days are over. Not at all. The steel chair is now used for attacks to the back and other more creative moves.

It's the "C" in "TLC" for a reason.

When you are in need of a place to sit, you don't have a lot of room, and comfort is nowhere near the top of your priority list then the steel chair is your friend.

However, that's not the case in professional wrestling.

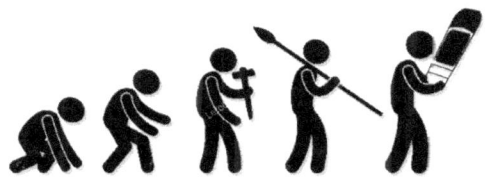

3. HISTORY

Wrestling has been around forever. Its origins are deep and has been around since ancient Greece.

But we're not going to go that far back today. We're just going to go about 200 years ago.

So, hop in your DeLorean, phone booth, Tardis, or preferred time traveling vehicle because it's time to...

Bump to the future.

In the 1830's the idea of combing wrestling and entertainment began in France.

It was connected to the sideshow attraction worlds of circuses, traveling carnivals, and vaudeville.

The traveling wrestling shows would continue to grow and be loved as a global art form and entertainment option.

At this time George Hackenschmidt, a thriving bodybuilder, began his illustrious and trailblazing career.

He would carry his share of championships, but also fame and acclaim.

Frank Gotch would become his biggest foe.

In 1911 the two would face off at Comiskey Park in Chicago and drew a very impressive 30,000 fans.

However, the form of professional wrestling as we know began in the 1920's. When the reveal of matches being predetermined became more widely known.

With the likes of Frank Gotch and Hackenschmidt retiring there just weren't any new stars at the time.

This led to Ed Lewis, Billy Sandow, and Toots Mondt joining forces to start their own promotion. This is where the wrestling as we know it in the modern day really took shape.

The innovative trio would feature tag team wrestling, time-limits, signature moves, and heel tactics like distracting the referee to add more theatrics life to the existing art form.

In 1948, the National Wrestling Alliance was born. The NWA was a group of independent companies that would unify their various world titles into to one "World Heavyweight" championship.

In the 1940's and 50's it would be Lou Thesz to lead the company.

In the 1950's, thanks to the invention of the television, professional wrestling saw a resurgence in popularly.

NWA would dominate for many years, but in 1960 Verne Gagne broke away from the alliance.

He renamed his company the American Wrestling Association and you could say the territory wars was in effect.
Vince McMahon Sr. Pulled his Capitol Wrestling Corporation from the NWA in 1963.

The 70's are best summed up with three things Bruno Sammartino, Andre' the Giant, and Georgia Championship Wrestling.

Sammartino would own the 60's while he held the WWWF Heavyweight Championship for seven years, eight months, and one day. That's 2,803 days.

He would win it back in 73, but in a huge disappointment he would only it for three years, four months, and twenty days this time. This man was truly a star.

Meanwhile another hall of famer was just getting started. Andre the Giant joined the WWWF in 1973. He would make the rounds through all of the territories as the legend of the giant truly began.

101 REASONS TO LOVE PRO WRESTLING

Then in 1979 Georgia Championship Wrestling would become the first nationally broadcast wrestling show on Ted Turner's TBS network. Wrestling on cable? Who would have thought?!

But this is still the same wrestling that was evolved through the carnival circuit. The carny tactics of trying to get over on someone was clearly at play.
They would one-up each other in attractions and the politics between rival overs over using wrestlers, money, and market dominance.

Enter Vince McMahon Jr. He would take over the WWF, buy national television slots, buy up territories, and become the leading brand in pro wrestling.

NWA would become centered around Jim Crockett Promotions and would finally land on TV in the mid-80's but it was too late to catch up to the momentum that Vince Jr.'s WWF had created.

A lot of that momentum is thanks to Hulk Hogan and WrestleMania.

Hogan became an icon and WrestleMania a past time.

The Rock n Wrestling Connection was a huge success to say the least.

For many, the 80's was a great period in history because of WWF's magic.

The WWF had the Immortal Hulk Hogan, the Eighth Wonder of the World Andre the Giant, Macho Man Randy Savage, and the Ultimate Warrior in singles while their tag division was stacked with the Hart Foundation, the British Bulldogs, and Demolition.

Meanwhile, NWA had the Nature Boy Ric Flair, the American Dream Dusty Rhodes, and Harley Race with the tag division likes of The Rock'n'Roll Express, The Midnight Express, The Four Horsemen duos, and the Road Warriors.

In the late 80's Jim Crockett would tap out and sell his NWA territory, the main one at the time, to TBS owner... Atlanta Braves owner... CNN owner... and Jane Fonda's husband... "Billionaire Ted" himself... Ted Turner.

In the first few years of ownership, he would rename the promotion to World Championship Wrestling.

101 REASONS TO LOVE PRO WRESTLING

WCW.

In 1993, WCW would break away from the NWA and do its own thing. And by own thing I mean hire WWF's biggest stars of the 80's.

The WWF would still hold their place as number one, but not by much.

While the legendary likes of the Undertaker, Shawn Michaels, and Bret Hart were having some fun feuds and rivalries the early to mid-90's was rough.

WCW couldn't do much with WWF's former stars but had established a strong under card and their homegrown main eventers were remarkable in the likes Sting, Ric Flair, and the Giant (which is not Andre but in fact the future WWE star the Big Show, who was being cast as Andre's alleged son.) Recreating WWF's 80's in the 90's just didn't work.

It would be a few years later and the next wave of WWF wrestlers to fall prey of Billionaire Ted Turner's deep pocketbooks. WWFs Diesel, Razor Ramon, 123 Kid, and a few others would jump ship to WCW.

This was all during the Monday Night Wars. WWFs Monday Night RAW and WCWs Monday Nitro were going head-to-head for ratings.

When Razor and Diesel showed up on Nitro, it created a gigantic - enormous - huge shift in ratings. For 83 weeks, WCW would dominate the ratings thanks to the New World Order.

The NWO became a pop culture hit thanks to a bad guy version of Hulk Hogan named "Hollywood" Hogan, Razor Ramon, who went by his real name of Scott Hall, and Kevin Nash who was Diesel in the WWF.

Meanwhile, Vince McMahon's WWF started to get a chip on its shoulder and begun their "Attitude Era". WWF struck lightening with the rise of "Stone Cold" Steve Austin, The Rock, Mick Foley's Mankind character, and everything just clicking at the same time. The wrestlers were pop culture icons, classic moments were created, and a lot of money was made.

Then digging deeper, on the East Coast there was Extreme Championship Wrestling. They were the third most successful company in the states.

Owned by Paul Heyman, ECW was the little engine that could. Well, the little engine that could swing a chair, dive from the balcony, incite a riot, and show you things you'd not see anywhere else.

ECW's hardcore style and a lot of what they did would quickly inspire WWF and WCW's products. And a good amount of ECW's top stars would leave for these company's bigger checkbooks and much larger exposure.

In 2001, the WWF bought both competitors WCW and ECW, becoming the juggernaut they are today.

In 2002, the World Wildlife Foundation sued the WWF over use of the initials WWF and actually won rights to the initials.

With that they got the F out and rebranded as the WWE.

The WWE would become a publicly traded company, go on to produce movies, and broke huge ground with their subscription service, the WWE Network.

The 2000's saw the rise of John Cena and Brock Lesnar as two true WWE Icons, but there was also likes of Triple H, Edge, Batista, Kurt Angle, and Randy Orton.

The 2010's have been dominated by the likes of Daniel Bryan, AJ Styles, and Roman Reigns while the WWE has seen its company become an entertainment juggernaut.

With no competition on a huge level, the WWE has been able to dominate the marketplace.

Companies like Ring of Honor and TNA... Impact... or whatever they want to be called have also put in the effort to compete. While these companies have had some outstanding talents, moments, and success in their own right, the WWE has reigned supreme.

In 2019, the group of Cody Rhodes, son of Dusty, the Young Bucks, and Kenny Omega joined forces with Tony Khan, the son of a billionaire businessman to launch All Elite Wrestling.

AEW would go on to join the WWE on a widely reached cable television platform as they bring pro wrestling back to Ted Turner's TNT network.

As we continue into a new decade, it is apparent that history repeats itself... even in professional wrestling.

101 REASONS TO LOVE PRO WRESTLING

This is JUST a tiny taste of the history of professional wrestling in America. Japan, Mexico, the UK, and other parts of the world have their own stories as well.

Folks on ESPN and in sports bars think it's impressive they know the batting average of some third baseman from four years ago. Hell, some even spout out knowledge from many years ago. It's baseball, basketball, football, hockey, etc.

You know what's even more impressive?

Knowing the name of all four members of the old biker gang stable "D.O.A." is impressive.

Knowing how many Intercontinental Title reigns Razor Ramon had is impressive.

There are many shows over many years with many memories, facts, stories, results, and moments.

You don't get much better than the history of wrestling.

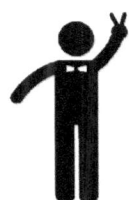

4. LAST MINUTE KICK OUTS

Before a child enters school, they know how to count to three.

The objective of professional wrestling matches is to win.

After wearing an opponent down, the wrestler will attempt to achieve victory.

The most traditional and common way is the pinfall.

A pinfall is when the wrestler has the other wrestler's shoulders pinned to the mat for a three count.

In pro wrestling, the referee will get down and physically count by slapping their hand on the mat.

1...

2...

But what if the wrestler kicks out?!

A kick out is when a wrestler lifts one or both of their pinned shoulders at the very moment the referee's authoritative hand is about to reach that oh so victorious three count.

The keyword is ABOUT to.

The silence of the anticipating crowd is interrupted by the spectacle of survival.

This is followed up by the collected eruption of awe and one of a few reactions.

A crowd will cheer if their favorite is the one who kicked out.

At the same rate, a bad guy will garner the opposite reaction.

Then there are times the athletic game of chess the two wrestlers are playing is so enthralling that they will be in amazement of the mere feat in front of them.

When a wrestler hits a big move and you just know it's over, the art of the last-minute kick out is enough to make the healthiest of hearts skip a beat.

It's a false finish. It's another chapter to the story. It's a sign of hope.

When two wrestlers enter the ring, anyone can have the hope of winning.

But that hope only becomes a reality when the referee counts

1...

2...

3.

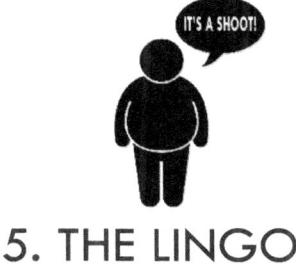

5. THE LINGO

The world of professional wrestling is unique, to say the least, and has been around a long time. With any long-running entity there are certain traditions and customs that are part of the story.

In professional wrestling, this includes an entire language.

Carny, or Kizarny, is the traditional language used between wrestlers that want to keep their conversation private from the fans.

It's called carny because that's where it comes from, the traveling carnival circuit of old.

It's like a cross between Pig Latin and Snoop's "izzle" talk. It sounds silly as hell and it is, but once you know it you "ciz-an't shizzake izzit."

On top of this wacky language, the world of wrestling has a plethora of terms that would make a non-fan raise more than the people's eyebrow.

Let's take a look at some of the basics:

Babyface: A "babyface" or simply a "face" is a good guy. The hero of the story. The goal of a face is to get the crowd on their side and yearn for their success.
Example: "The babyface's comeback delighted the crowd."

Heel: The "heel" is a villain. The bad guy. They will cheat, antagonize the crowd, and their success is measured in boos.
Example: "The heel made the children cry as she cheated their hero out of victory."

Booker: A booker, or "writer" in some cases, is the creative mind behind the fun. They plot out the story lines, matches, and moments.
Example: "The booking on this show has gone downhill."

Over: When a wrestler has achieved their goal of connecting with the crowd as a face or heel. The audience has bought in to their gimmick to the point of genuine reaction.
Example: "The new wrestler's improvements have got him over with the crowd."

Job: To job is to lose a match. An extension of this is a "jobber", which is someone who always loses matches in order to help put others over.
Example: "The small wrestler had to job to the bigger wrestler who needed the win."

Bump: To fall down. This is often in reaction to another wrestler giving the other a move or in attempt to hurt one's opponent. Along with grappling holds and strikes, these are the crashing falls that wears the wrestlers down.
Example: "The fall from the cage was a horrible bump."

Selling: The art of acting out the pain of a move, the surprise of a story line twist, or written plot points. It is the performance that convinces the audience that the predetermined action is believable.
Example: "After the show, the wrestler continued to sell his leg injury with a limp."

Promo: A promo is an in-character speech, interview, or monologue that is used to garner the wrestler, a story line, or match more attention, anticipation, or suspense.
Example: "The promo that wrestler just cut got the crowd excited for the match."

Work: A "work" is when something is fake or scripted. It's when the performer is on script and participating in the agreed-upon illusion.
Example: That's not a real injury! That's a work!"

Shoot: A "shoot" is when something is real or unscripted. This can be done verbally in a "shoot promo", where the performer breaks the fourth wall and exposes the business. Or someone can physically "shoot", which is as you can correctly assume is when a wrestler attempts to legitimately hurt their opponent.
Example: "From the looks of her bloody nose, you would think they were shooting."

Blading: The blood you see in professional wrestling is not always from a violent collision, but it does happen. It's often uncontrolled and is taken very serious by medical staff. However, more so in the past, professional wrestler would go that extra extreme step in order to thrill a crowd.

No, that's not ketchup.

Blading, or gigging, is the act of cutting one's own body, often the crown of the forehead, to achieve the gruesome effect of blood.
Example: "The veteran wrestler's forehead is covered in scars from years of blading."

Mark: A "mark" is a fan of professional wrestling. It is often used as an insult, but anyone who is a fan of pro wrestling can be considered a "mark".

There are also "smarks" or "smart marks" who follow the backstage politics and consider themselves educated on the business.

With the access of information that is the internet, the lines of "mark" and "smark" have been blurred.

Ultimately, Fans are marks and marks are fans.

Example: "The mark held their up high in attempt to anger the bad guy."

And finally... **Kayfabe**.

Kayfabe is the all-encompassing term that maintains the suspension of disbelief. It is sticking to the script, staying in character, and playing along.

Example: "The rival wrestlers stopped conversing when they spotted a mark nearby to avoid breaking kayfabe."

The lingo of professional wrestling goes on and on.

All of this is "insider talk", but pretty much anyone who follows wrestling can tell you a good chunk of the lingo.

It's just kind of cool that we have our own language.

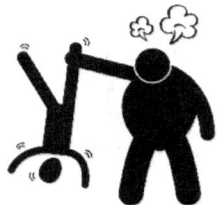

6. DAVID VS. GOLIATH

The lore of a smaller man taking on the impossible challenge of facing off with a giant has been around since the beginning of time

The term itself goes back to the biblical story of David, a normal man, defeating a nine-foot giant soldier by slinging stones at him and then cutting his head off.

While no one in professional wrestling is cutting heads off, thankfully, there are many stories and examples of the underdog rising to that oh so impossible challenge.

There is minimal hope for a man who is dwarfed by feet, not inches, and hundreds and hundreds of pounds.

The behemoths of old would rarely even bump for anyone, that alone a smaller man.

And why would they?

They were massive in comparison to their opponents.

Yet, the spectacle that is the sight of a giant looking downward on the little guy is a staple in the sport.

Common sense doesn't mean we, the fans, are forced to automatically cheer the bigger guy.

This is professional wrestling! We have our own rules and reality.

With a little creativity, everyone has a chance.

The Davids of professional wrestling might not always slay the beast, but sometimes leave them worn and with a newfound respect for the smaller man.

But sometimes, sometimes miracles can happen.

Sometimes the Goliath isn't taken down by a well slung stone to the forehead.

Sometimes the Goliath doesn't get their head cut off.

Sometimes the Goliath isn't defeated by prayer, but rather by chair!

Sometimes it's a big move.

Sometimes it's utilizing one's quickness to sneak in the pin.

Glorified giant killers like lucha legend Rey Mysterio, hall of famer "1-2-3 Kid" Sean Waltman, ECW icon Spike Dudley, and the enigma Jeff Hardy have all proved that not only can a smaller wrestler hang with the monsters, but sometimes, actually win.

In professional wrestling, big things CAN come in small packages.

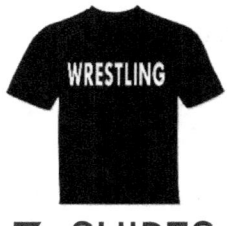

7. SHIRTS

The T-Shirt as we know is said to first appear during the Spanish-American War when the U.S. Navy issued them to soldiers as underwear.

Over time, the T-Shirt would become acceptable as casual outerwear.

Printed T-Shirts would debut in the 1940's, but it wouldn't be until the 60's when the printed T-Shirt would become a cultural norm.

With their finger on the pulse of pop culture, professional wrestlers would inevitably adopt the new form of self-expression.

The 60's and 70's saw some very memorable uses of the printed text T-Shirt.

Whether it was one of Ox Baker's bluntly heel "YOU WILL HATE ME" shirt.

Or the "DUSTY SUCKS EGGS" shirt Terry Funk wore to antagonize the famous Son of a Plumber. In case you didn't know his father's occupation, Dusty Rhodes confirmed this with his own shirt.

Then in the late 1970's, Greg Valentine was so proud of his destruction of the late great "Chief" Wahoo McDaniel that he sported a "I BROKE WAHOOS LEG" shirt to garner heat.

With the rise of the WWF in the 80's, everyone started getting shirts to both wear as part of their identity, but also sell to the fans as souvenirs and a chance to represent their favorite superstars.

The wrestling business and the world would quickly learn that wrestling fans don't wear their hearts on their sleeves, they wear their hearts on the whole damn shirt.

During the 80's, we saw shirts like Hulk Hogan's iconic yellow and red "Hulkamania" shirt, "Rowdy" Roddy Piper's "Hot Rod" ringer shirt, and Randy Savage's awesome "Macho Man" shirt.

The 90's would see two other massively successful shirts in "Stone Cold" Steve Austin's "Austin 3:16" shirt and the New World Order's "nWo" logo shirt.

Still, everyone with value got shirts made or even multiple shirts.

And the fans of wrestling bought them all.

The WWF and WCW weren't the only ones cranking out successful shirts.

It wouldn't be too surprising to see Cactus Jack's "Wanted Dead" shirt or any of the ECW shirts in the 90's and early 2000's.

The 2000's can be summed up with two shirts: CM Punk's very successful white shirt with lightning bolts and the Bullet Club shirt. This shirt was brought into Hot Topics by consumer demand thanks to the soaring popularity of the New Japan Pro Wrestling stable.

In recent years, the merchandise market has not slowed down.

The WWE cranks out new shirts almost weekly.

Meanwhile, as fashion often dictates... what was once old, is now retro.

And thanks to technology and very smart business, there are even options for the independent performers to sell their shirts online and at shows.

Everyone has a shirt!

They say the kindest of people would give you the shirt off their back.

However, if it's an "Austin 3:16" shirt, a professional wrestling fan might not be so kind.

101 REASONS TO LOVE PRO WRESTLING

8. DRAMA

Everyone has a story.

One they've experienced themselves, one they have been told by others, or one they've made up completely out of thin air.

To tell their narrative, a decision is to be made on what style and tone to deliver it in.

The use of drama to captivate an audience is a timeless tradition.

It's a serious tone of storytelling that utilizes a wide range of emotions and unexpected circumstances.

As one would imagine, the brawler's ballet that is professional wrestling is not without a colossal amount of drama.

Based on Aristotle's "Six Elements of Drama", professional wrestling passes all of the requirements with flying colors and probably a few flying elbow drops.

First and most importantly is **PLOT**. The plot is considered most important of Aristotle's artistic criteria.

For a dramatic story to have a lasting effect, it needs a great plot, or a collection of moments, that present the arc of the story.

To say wrestling hasn't had its share of iconic story lines would be an understatement.

When a plot is well written and well performed the viewer is rewarded with an escape from reality that can sometimes have more impact on them than their actual daily lives.

The second of the six is **SPECTACLE**. Professional wrestling IS spectacle.

It's the "ooo" and the "awe". It's the roller coaster of emotion.

The biggest of dramas ends in the biggest of matches. Two competitors finally going face to face to settle their issues in a ring in front of invested spectators. If this isn't a spectacle, I don't know what is.

Third is **CHARACTER**. This is not only the gimmick, but the moral compass of the performers. It is who the players of the story essentially are.

We have humble heroes, evil villains, those born with a silver spoon in their mouths, and those from the wrong side of the tracks. There's everything in between. All for the audience to relate with, associate with, and even despise.

Next is **DICTION**. Diction is the speech style. It's the chosen tone and style to deliver a message. It can be common speech or something poetic.

No matter the delivery, if the audience is captivated the performer's job is being done.

Fifth is **THOUGHT**. This is the philosophy behind the lesson being told. It's the acknowledgment of roles and the presented reality. It's good defeating evil. It's insecurity of the heart. It's jealousy. It's what ignites the passion of the character and gives the audience the decision of what side to choose.

And finally, **MELODY** is the background score to the story. It's the rhythm and pacing of punctuating the right points and unleashing the perfect tempo of tempers.

In both the story line and in the actual matches themselves, this is the give and pull between the performers and the audience that brings emotion to a boiling point.

It's an artistic understanding of manipulating the crowd's collective emotions.

The pulse of the professional wrestling industry is etched in the blood, sweat, and tears of created drama.

Aristotle was a visionary, a scientist, and the father of western philosophy. But even he wouldn't have imagined the drama crafted by professional wrestling.

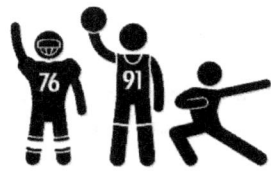

9. PRO ATHLETE CROSSOVERS

The history of pro wrestling crossovers goes back to the 1910's when Jack Johnson, a renowned boxer, entered the world of wrestling.

Since then, professional wrestling has had a storied past with professional athletes crossing over to the beloved squared circle.

Everyone with a little muscle and success in athletics thinks they could be destined for the same success, but it's not always a sure shot.

There are essentially three kinds of pro athlete cross overs.

The first of the three are those who show up for a big one-off match.

They will show up and promote the big event and do their best to not embarrass themselves while entertaining.

The likes of Muhammad Ali would battle Antonio Inoki and even referee the main event of Wrestle Mania 1.

At WrestleMania 2, members of the Chicago Bears NFL team would take part in a huge 20-Man Battle Royal.

Of course, who could forget the appearances by commentator Bob Uecker and Pete Rose.

Big examples of a cross over athlete having the big mat would be "LT" Lawrence Taylor taking on Bam Bam Bigelow in the main event of WrestleMania 11.

In 1997, NBA Champion, and apparent American ambassador, Dennis Rodman joined the nWo during the peak of their success.

Then of course, Floyd "Money" Mayweather taking on The Big Show at WrestleMania 24.

Some of these moments are classics that fans will never forget. Some are moments that wrestling fan nightmares are made of.

The second type of pro athlete cross overs are those who want to capitalize on their professional sports fame.

These performers come in, train, and honestly put in the effort to succeed.

But sadly, this category is for those who were unsuccessful in their attempt to sincerely crossover.

NFL Hall of Famer Kevin Greene joined WCW and could have potentially done more but had to exit the world of wrestling once the NFL insisted on no-wrestling clauses in contracts.

2007 saw Adam "Pacman" Jones showing up in TNA and due to his NFL contract dictating that he can have no physical contact hit was thus pointless. This didn't stop TNA from giving him the TNA Tag Titles alongside Ron "R-Truth" Killings.

In 2013, Quinten Rampage Jackson joined the TNA roster to surprisingly less than stellar reviews. He would ditch wrestling to go back to fighting.

There have been many pro athlete cross overs that we are best to just forget.

The final type of pro athlete crossovers are those who truly excel.

These athletes enter the world of professional wrestling, and they just get it.

They blend right into the beautiful sonata that is professional wrestling.

They connect with the crowd, they win championships, and they create hall of fame legacies.

We're talking about the household names like Brock Lesnar and Kurt Angle. Those who had success in collegiate and Olympic style wrestling but would find their careers take off in the squared circle.

The Rock, Ron Simmons, Goldberg, Titus O'Neil, and a slew of others came from the world of football.

Ken Shamrock, Dan Severn, Matt Riddle, and Rhonda Rousey came from UFC and have had their own success respectively.

Before Mark Henry was inducting his opponents into the "hall of pain" he was an Olympic weightlifter.

The list of successful pro athlete cross overs in wrestling goes on and on.

And continues to grow in the current landscape.

A pro athlete may be able to score the winning touchdown, thrill the crowd with a slam dunk, or get the knockout with one epic punch.

Nevertheless, the world of professional wrestling requires a unique breed of athlete to effectively crossover.

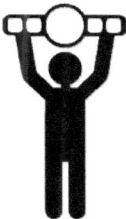

10. CHAMPIONSHIP BELTS

Small-minded people will mock professional wrestling by minimizing the art form to two grown adults in their underwear fighting over a belt.

But we know better.

A championship belt is a symbol of greatness.

The first championship belt was awarded to bare-knuckle boxer Tom Cribb in 1810 by King George III after a victory over a slave. So, there's that...

The roots of the championship belt in professional wrestling dates back to 1905 when George Hackenschmidt became recognized as the World champion after winning tournaments in various countries.

In professional wrestling, the wrestlers fight back and forth, clawing and climbing up the rankings giving it their all and then some.

Just so they can be handed over the title belt after an epic win.

The belt is king. The craftsmanship, the feel of holding it, and the cool look of a cool belt is undeniable. The evolution of these amazingly well-crafted pieces of combative art has been truly breath-taking.

Along with the classic World Champion, wrestling has had many other titles include the Tag Team Titles, titles for specific weight divisions, and other secondary mid-card belts.

These belts would have designs obvious to their designation.

Some would even prefer these belts over the design of the respected World strap.

The championship belt would change with the times.

From smaller to bigger, from dull to shiny, and from basic to very detailed.

The most renowned of all iconic championship belts is the "Big Gold Belt". This magnificently constructed belt was crafted by silversmith Charles Crumrine. It saw its legacy go back to the Jim Crockett era of NWA, would be part of WWF folklore when "Nature Boy" Ric Flair showed up with it in 1991, and would be used by the WWE during a few of the many brand split eras.

From 1976 to 1986, the NWA used the original "10 pounds of gold". This piece had a very precise design that features a domed earth center piece with beautifully constructed flags of different nations. With the resurgence of NWA, the 10 pounds of gold has returned to the spotlight once again.

In 1988, at WrestleMania III, the WWF introduced their "Winged Eagle" design. This awe-inspiring design was part of many fan's childhoods as the likes of Hulk Hogan, "Macho Man" Randy Savage, Bret "The Hitman" Hart, the Undertaker, Shawn Michaels, and Steve Austin would all have all held this design before the company would move on during the peak of the Attitude era.

In recent years the WWF has removed a lot of the personality of these championships in favor of a more universal design style. It might as well be tattooed around the waist of Brock Lesnar or Roman Reigns.

Meanwhile, there are other stunning straps, tremendous titles, and beautiful belts out there being earned, yearned, and heralded in their own respect.

Yes, at the end of the day, a championship belt could be considered a prop.

But like Freddy's glove, Ralphie's BB Gun, and Dorothy's Ruby reds… it can mean a whole lot.

The belt is the coolest championship in sports.

The championship belt is history.

It's a symbol of success.

It's the epitome of achievement.

This is something any fan of professional wrestling would gladly defend.

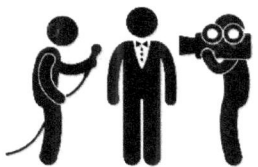

11. DEBUTS WITH VIGNETTES

The word vignette comes from the French and means "little vine".

In theatre, literature, and in professional wrestling a vignette is a short presentation used to introduce the audience to a new character or characters that will soon be added to the mix.

The cast of crazy characters in wrestling is infinite, but some characters need some explaining before they invade the world, the ring, and our minds.

Thanks to vignettes, a performer debuting into a company for the first time or a performer debuting a new persona can make an impact before even taking a single bump.

We see who they are. What they are about. Their initial motivations for joining the roster.

Some of these are simple and to the point, others are more ominous, and others are just weird.

The 90's saw horrible gimmicks eat up airtime but there were some solid characters rolled out.

Mr. Perfect showcased his athletic perfection with a series of memorable videos.

The bizarre one, Goldust, brought us a taste of Hollywood.

IRS, Irwin R Schyster, gave us tax cheats the tips to get on law-biding path.

J - E - Double F, J - A- Double R - E - Double T, Jeff Jarrett showed us what it took to be a country music star.

Chris Jericho would enter the WWF in 1999 via the legendary "Countdown to the Millennium" clock that would ominously appear for months leading up to zero.

Edge's moody-Blade-like introduction videos were actually cool and gave his debut an added boost.

In the late 2010's, fans of professional wrestling have been treated to some very compelling character pieces.

The introduction of Jon Moxley getting out of his proverbial WWE shackles and entering the world of All Elite Wrestling.

And then there's Bray Wyatt's transformation from cult leader, which itself had some great intros, to the host of the Firefly Fun House and The Fiend.

And then some character vignettes in professional wrestling just wouldn't connect.

Either they don't make sense, or the character isn't as marketable as anticipated.

Some just don't get a chance like Billy Jack Haynes in the 80's, Sean O'Haire's "Devil's Advocate" character, or the NXT stand-out stable of Sanity… but others just flat out flopped.

They attempted to capitalize on the success of Crocodile Dundee with Outback Jack.

The 90's gave us the Repo Man taking people's stuff, Waylon Mercy being awesomely creepy, and Dean Douglas failing out of the WWF not too long after debuting.

The 2000's have not been innocent of failed attempts either.

Thankfully some talents can reinvent themselves despite the introduction they are given.

Kofi Kingston came in with a Jamaican accent and would later be added to a soulful group of New Day. This was nowhere close to the New Day the world came to love.

Some vignettes actually create more questions than answers…

Who would want to remember Beaver Cleavage?

What was WCW thinking with the redebut of the former Goldust, Dustin Rhodes, with the kind of questionable intro videos for the new character Seven?

When were we ever going to see Emmalina debut despite vignettes airing forever?

And really, what was Glacier going to do after thawing out?

So many questions, so little time....

Becoming a star in professional wrestling is like capturing lightning in a bottle.

Sometimes that lightning strikes because the star's debut was well-hyped with exceptional vignette videos.

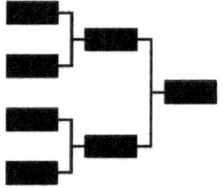

12. TOURNAMENTS

The term tournament goes back to the medieval times, where it was used to describe a combatant going through a series of events.

Today tournaments are used for everything from Poker championships, video game competitions, and even Jeopardy has "Tournaments of Champions".

The use of tournaments is mostly associated with sports.

Most notably, the NCAA's annual basketball championship tournament.

Its roots go back to 1939 with Oregon winning to the month-long event now known as March Madness.

In professional wrestling we see the field of competitors start off with 8, 16, or even 32 in some cases and through in-ring war shrink down to a final two.

There have been tournaments in professional wrestling for centuries, but Japanese Wrestling Association's "World Big League" tournament set the standard.

From 1959 through 1972, this tournament was dominated by Rikidozen, who by luck, also owned JWA.

The JWA would shut down and New Japan Pro Wrestling's "G1 Climax" tournament would take the tournament ball and run with it. This tournament would give us many dream matches and memorable winners.

The WWF would go on to create "King of the Ring". Starting in 1985, the "King of the Ring" has established many WWF stars on their way to icon status. It would come and go but has returned in 2019 with a victory by Baron Corbin.

The 80's would also introduce us to the "Crockett Cup" tournament. NWA's best competed in a tag team tournament from 86 to 88. This historic tournament has returned with the NWA renaissance of the late 2010's.

The independent promotions have also seen great success with their own annual tournaments. ECWA's long-time running "Super 8" tournament was a measuring stick of greatness and keeps going today.

There's PWG's "Battle of Los Angeles", Chikara's "King of Trios" tournament, and more consistently putting out great elimination-style tournaments every year.

Tournaments aren't always an annual event.

Sometimes a tournament is used to showcase new stars or new ideas. Sometimes a tournament crowns the first champion of a new division. Sometimes a tournament decides the top contender.

Sometimes a tournament fills a void to crown a vacant champion. As is the case with WrestleMania IV, which saw "Macho Man" Randy Savage outlast 13 other WWF superstars to become WWF World Champion.

Then the same championship would need to be filled again at the 1998 Survivor Series pay per view. This memorable tournament saw some great matches that would inevitably lead to The Rock winning and joining The Corporation.

Tournaments can be great. At the same rate, they could be something we would rather forget.

Everyone is hungry for tournaments as declared in Chicago's "RedEye" magazine's "Best Sandwich" tournament. This can be washed down with Detroit Free Press's "Michigan Brewery Madness" tournament. All while taking in LA Week's "Best LA Novel Ever" tournament.

We love tournaments. They are the playoffs. It's the end of the season and the road to the championship.

Professional wrestling tournaments give us unexpected dream matches with unexpected results, surprising upsets, heroes crowned, glimpses into the future, and history being written.

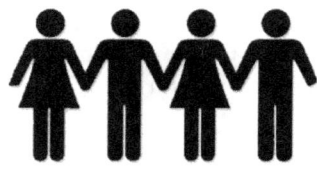

13. DIVERSITY

Diversity is the spice of life.

There is a plethora of colors, and they all have their place in the crayon box of life.

We are given the choice of size in most situations because people have different preferences.

Just like crayons and coffee, people come in different colors and different sizes.

It's a beautiful world when you think about it. Our society has different sexes, nationalities, creeds, cultures, and lineages that make up the human race.

Professional wrestling is no different.

Professional wrestlers come in all sorts of shapes, all sorts of sizes, heroes of all races, bad asses of all sexes, of all creeds, of all orientations, and of all cultures.

Yes, professional wrestling is one big happy family.

But let's not ignore the elephant in the room.

Just like world history, there are horrible truths that should not be ignored.

Professional wrestling has been plagued by stereotypical characters where the foreign characters were always evil, cultures mocked, entire races parodied, and some very offensive depictions.

But again, like society, professional wrestling is no different. The upward battle against discrimination has been a struggle.

101 REASONS TO LOVE PRO WRESTLING

In the late 1950's when America still had segregated water fountains, professional wrestling had Sputnik Monroe. A white man who did not care about race at all and would even be cited a $25 fine for "mopery" or hanging out with African Americans.

In the early 70's, Monroe would even go on to form one of the first mixed-race tag teams as he teamed up with Norvell Austin, a black man, to much dismay of close-minded fans and industry alike.

Sputnik's integrity and the pure talents of the likes of Bobo Brazil would pave the way for future greatness.

Thanks to black female wrestling pioneers like Ramona Isbell, who was good enough to entertain southern fans but not enough to eat in their restaurants, today's modern stars can strive.

With initiatives like WWE's "Women's Revolution", the 2010's have seen professional wrestling make gigantic waves to feature everyone.

All Elite Wrestling is another great example of a newer promotion completely ignoring the ways of old to pave a new all-inclusive path.

Stereotypes are becoming further and further behind us.

Barriers have not only been knocked down, but knocked out.

Any culture can be Champ.

Whoever YOU are can be represented.

Professional wrestling fans embrace all cultures. We don't care about your personal life. We don't care if you're from the northern border or the southern border. We don't care about your religious beliefs. We don't care if you're a French giant or a ravishing Russian. We don't care if you pump a fist or take a bow.

Take pride in your roots. Stand tall. Stand united.

Because at the end of the day, the fans of professional wrestling are listening.

The world is watching.

If someone says something that pushes us back, the world definitely hears it.

When you're popular in wrestling you're considered "over", and that itself is colorblind.

History has proven that what matters most is the connection between the performer and the crowd.

When you're over, you're over.

And after the bell sounds at the end of a great match, a professional wrestling fan just wants to be entertained.

14. ENTRANCE MUSIC

Music is considered the universal art.

It's something that all ears can share in, experience, and enjoy.

It's a pulse of melodic energy, a contagious beat, a tantalizing tempo.

To capitalize on these emotion-inducing tunes, a long-time tradition in professional wrestling is entrance music.

When entering ringside, a professional wrestler is often accompanied by their own signature entrance music.

The moment this music hits the anticipating crowd automatically knows how to react.

It could be a classic composition like Ric Flair's epic entrance to "Also sprach Zarathustra", "Macho Man" Randy Savage's "Pomp and Circumstance", or Daniel Bryan's use of "Flight of the Valkyries".

It could be an upbeat jam, a slow-tempo song, or just about anything that strikes an emotional chord with the crowd.

It could be any genre of music. Wrestling is often fueled by rock and roll, but the options are limitless.

West Texas Rednecks and the Godwinns gave us memorable country themes.

Hip Hop has seen representation by the likes of John Cena, Mark Henry, and New Jack.

Let's not forget about immaculate classical compositions like Mr. Perfect's perfect music, Shinsuke Nakamura's violin classic, or the screeching guitars of Bret "The Hitman" Hart's theme.

101 REASONS TO LOVE PRO WRESTLING

ECW gave us everything cool about the 90's.

There have been boy bands, funk, opera, disco, and everything in between.

A lot of these classic songs have been created by three eras of musicians.

The 80's saw Hall of Fame manager Jimmy Hart dazzle the keys for the entrances of Honky Tonk Man, Dusty Rhodes, Legion of Doom and more.

Jim Johnston created some of the best themes of all time during the 90's and 2000's. We're talking "Stone Cold" Steve Austin, The Rock, Mr. McMahon, and hundreds more we all hum in private.

And then the C.F.O.'s knocked out some of latest hits of the 2010's with instant classics like Bobby Roode's "Glorious", Kevin Owen's "Fight", Asuka's "The Future", and Boom-bastic entrance for the Undisputed Era to name a few.

When you hear that glass break, feel the haunting aura of the funeral bells dong, or rise to your feet at the opening notes of "Burn It Down", you know exactly who is coming through that curtain.

You know exactly how to respond.

These works of audio-expression have made lasting generational impressions so it would be remiss to not take a moment to recognize the lyrical brilliance of professional wrestling entrance songs.

So, I close this with what I call an ode to the Entrance Theme...

Look in my eyes, what do you see?

You think you know me?

I can slap a tornado. I can dry up a sea.

I hear voices in my head. They talk to me.

Everybody's got a price.

Everybody's gonna pay.

Badstreet Atlanta-GA., Baddest street in the whole USA.

101 REASONS TO LOVE PRO WRESTLING

I come from tomorrow to take back today.

Feel the power. Today is a New Day.

Who's that jumpin' out the sky?

When it comes smashing down and it hurts inside.

It's a mystery I don't know why.

If you ever take a trip down to Cobb County, Georgia, ya betta read the signs.

Somebody gonna get their wig split.

Cuz' it's all about the game and how you play it.

Their knees get weak. Whenever I'm around.

Bow to the masters, break it down.

Oh, you didn't know?

Spend my day working hard on the go.

Unlike the Mounties we always get our man.

And we're off to never-never land.

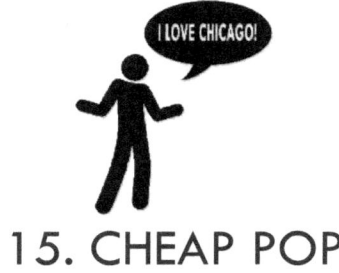

15. CHEAP POP

The act of pandering to an audience has been part of sales going back to snail oil salesmen, ill-intended preachers, and snake-in-the-grass politicians.

It's gratification of the masses in a non-genuine gesture or declaration.

It's an attempt to appeal to a crowd and draw support by telling what they want to hear.

In professional wrestling, this is the cheap pop.

The pop is the eruption of emotion from the crowd.

It is the roaring reaction to the situation at hand.

A cheap pop is when a wrestler incites a positive reaction from the crowd by using a cheesy tactic.

Basically, the wrestler does whatever it takes to kiss the crowd's collective rear end.

And it works.

We, fans, become creatures of habit. We come to the show to see the show.

This means we have no issue in participating in cheap pop rituals.

Many wrestlers would pander with patriotism.

Everyone loves the hometown hero.

It's easy to get a crowd of people with similar interests to take notice.

There is no way a crowd can hate someone who is being nice to the kids.

No one can boo a guy supporting the same local sports team they support.

The chances of getting boos when the crowd sees a wrestler hanging out with a big star is pretty slim.

Ron Simmons gets the cheap pop with one damn word.

The crowd just likes to interact.

Whether it's throwing up a Daniel Bryan "Yes", a "too-sweet" hand symbol, or "Wooing" after a chop professional wrestling knows exactly what buttons to press to electrify a crowd.

When a rockstar comes to town and tells the adoring crowd that their city is the best, it's no different than The Rock finally coming back to (place city here), Mick Foley being thrilled to be right in in (place city here), or Scott Hall asking (place city here) if they are there to see the nWo.

If it helps the wrestler make one extra person cheer them on and it doesn't hurt anyone, there is nothing wrong with a little indulgence of instinct.

101 REASONS TO LOVE PRO WRESTLING

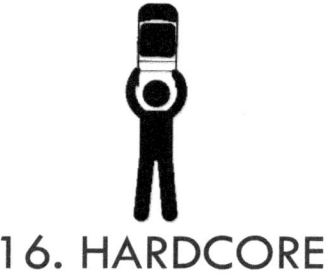

16. HARDCORE

The noun hardcore has a few meanings.

It's the most active or committed members of a group or movement.

It's also defined as explicit and extreme.

In professional wrestling the term hardcore is mostly reserved for the use of weapons in an extreme manner in order to claim a victory.

However, the use of weapons in battle is not exclusive to professional wrestling.

Accessorized combat has been around since cavemen learned that rocks do indeed hurt.

There is even hardcore fighting in the bible. The world's most bestselling book features axes, bow and arrows, clubs, daggers, maces, slings, spears, and swords.

Weapon usage can even be considered a high art.

In professional wrestling there have been no holds barred and hardcore matches since the 1950's and 60's. These brawls would be under street fight, cage, and bull rope match rules among others.

In most cases, a hardcore stipulation is reserved to settle a long-term blood feud. But some wrestlers turned these not-so-random acts of violence into their identity and norm.

This would evolve across the world as the likes of The Sheik, Abdulla "The Butcher", Carlos Colon, Terry Funk, and Bruiser Brody all made names for themselves and their promotions by going to physical extremes to thrill the crowd.

In the late 80's, FMW was formed. A Japanese based company with a focus on death matches.

Then in the 1990's, came Extreme Championship Wrestling. A company that became an American alternative that focused on blood.

With the likes of the "Homicidal, Suicidal, and Genocidal" Sabu, "The Original Gangsta" New Jack, and of course the "Hardcore Legend" Cactus Jack to name a few that paved the way.

ECW's edgy content would influence the WWF's "Attitude Era".

WWF jumped on the hardcore bandwagon with the use of tables, ladders, chairs, trash cans, shopping carts and even sledgehammers and mannequin heads.

And in modern times, these weapons are still being used with equal opportunity for carnage.

At the same time, the death match counterculture and hardcore tributes are just as prominent today.

After ECW, companies like IWA Mid-South, Xtreme Pro Wrestling or XPW, and CZW have carried the hardcore and death match baton.

In the latest evolutions of hardcore, GCW, or Game Changer Wrestling, has stepped up the plate. They are not shy to use barbed wire, violent contraptions, and even beds of nails.

Hardcore is still part of the mainstream.

All Elite Wrestling does not seem to hesitate in using graphic violence and staple gunned cigarettes to get eyes on the product.

Impact Wrestling has a hardcore edge to it too and, obviously, so did the House of Hardcore promotion. A company ran by the Innovator of Violence himself, Tommy Dreamer.

We professional wrestling fans can get a little wild sometimes, but sometimes it can go a little too far.

The stunned emotion of a crimson mask is part of our legacy.

But that's what it's all about, hardcore is emotion. And sometimes that emotion is psychotic.

It's doing whatever it takes to take out your opponent, even at one's own physical expense.

True fans know that hardcore isn't just swinging weapons and blood.

It's an attitude of simply not giving a damn.

It's a way of life.

But if there's a weapon in hand, anyone can be hardcore.

101 REASONS TO LOVE PRO WRESTLING

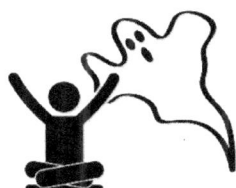

17. EVERY DAY IS HALLOWEEN

The history of Halloween can be told in many forms, but in general, it's a night to dress up into any costume you want and have a good time.

You can be anything for Halloween. From jokers, smokers, and midnight tokers to a puppet, a pauper, a pirate, a poet, a pawn, and a king. From Sinatra to Steve Miller.

And this is perfectly okay because like the industrial metal pioneers Ministry so boldly proclaimed, "to me every day is Halloween"

In professional wrestling the idea of a Halloween-worthy character would evolve from the use of nicknames like "The Hammer", "The Lion", or other circus-inspired gimmicks.

This carny-loving world of wrestling would always have the oddball characters, the so-called freaks, and the monsters step in for a renewed spotlight.

These zany characters would come and go without ever leading a territory or taking on a World-level championship.

This would carry on into the 1980's as the WWF ignited a character boom of "Warriors", "Tornados", "Tugboats", "Immortals", and "Police Officers".

Meanwhile, WCW and elsewhere weren't shy to give it a go as well.

For better or for worse, these characters are part of history and were part of the current pop culture at the time.

Then at in the early 90's the WWF put their top title on The Undertaker. It was short lived, but it opened hells gates to legitimize the possibilities of any character being champion.

Down south, WCW was also starting to soar with the face-painted surfer named Sting being established as a top guy.

The 90's would give us many treats in the form of spooky, eccentric, and fun characters.

With every treat comes the trick as the 90's wasn't so kind for some.

If engraved mental images of the Dungeon of Doom didn't steal your candy bag already, you got your eggs and toilet paper aimed for some of their tricks of the 2000's.

We were also treated to the likes of The Boogeyman, a high-flying bunny, and other poisonous characters.

And like every era, the 2000's have given us genuinely fun and interesting oddballs, so-called freaks, and monsters.

They say the freaks come out at night, but if a wrestling show is booked for the afternoon, then, by God, the freaks come out in the afternoon.

At the end of the night, we all take in our haul of candy. Some of it is great, but there is also a large portion of non-edible nonsense. We still wouldn't trade the experience for the world.

It's easy to understand why a fan of pro wrestling would want every day to be Halloween, or at least a few weeknights a week and a Sunday or two a month.

18. THE HOT TAG

There have been many famous duos that have each other's backs through thick and thin.

There's Batman and Robin.

Lennon and McCartney.

Jake and Elwood.

Bert and Ernie.

As is the case in professional wrestling.

The addition of tag team wrestling has been around since the beginning of the modern sport.

These traditionally two-on-two match ups are an opportunity for the fans to cheer a tandem and for the performer to share the creative experience with another wrestler.

The hot tag occurs when one of the good guys has been beaten up so long by the dastardly duo that the moment their desperately extended hand tags their partner the crowd erupts.

The anxiously rested partner enters the ring and essentially beats up both bad guys, thus ending their evil momentum.

This instance provides the crowd with hope as a well-done hot tag gets them to their feet with adrenaline matching the freshly tagged competitor.

There have been some iconic tag teams through professional wrestling history.

101 REASONS TO LOVE PRO WRESTLING

The likes of Harlem Heat, the Road Warriors, the Hart Foundation, The Rock and Roll Express, the Hardy Boyz, The Rockers, Edge and Christian, the Steiner Brothers, the Dudley Boys, New Age Outlaws, the Young Bucks, the Briscoes, the Usos, the New Day, and hundreds more that are either in the Hall of Fame or definitely worthy of the high honor.

Of course, a great persona and great rivals go into achieving this level of acclaim.

However, a large part of what makes a tag team great is great matches.

Some have had success because of big memorable moments, but when it is broken down to the basics, it's all about the hot tag.

A professional wrestling match can be grueling enough.

Add another opponent and it can be torturous.

As fans, we watch our favorite superstars get worn down, beaten down, and dominated by the great heels.

We slowly find ourselves at the edges of our seats.

Our fingernails start to dwindle down.

Our hopes solely rest in the feat of the face in peril reaching his partner for the tag.

Then those dastardly heels cut him off.

But we keep waiting.

We cheer for this performer to reach their partner and at that specific moment in time nothing else in the outside world matters.

And just as our faith truly starts to be tested, it happens.

The hot tag.

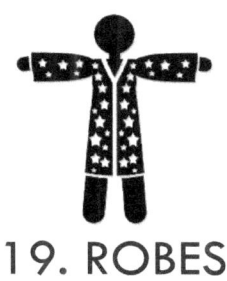

19. ROBES

There is an overabundance of clothing items that a professional fighter can wear to the ring.

Many of the greats have gone with the entrance robe.

A robe is a loose-fitting outer garment with many purposes. It can be part of academia regalia, worn as a judge, religious dress, rocked in royalty, in fantasy literature, and it's a conveniently warm option for exiting the bath, swimming, or in sports, exiting the locker room.

The walk from the locker room can be pretty long.

Sometimes the warmth of a robe is called for to maintain warmth from a pre-fight warm up.

And there is no reason these robes cannot be magnificent works of fashionable art.

Robes have been part of professional wrestling from the very beginning of the sport and in all countries. These no-frills robes were worn by some of the greatest of the black and white era.

Also, during this time, the incorporation of glamour can be credited to the flamboyant Gorgeous George. His robes were unlike his predecessors as they were part of his act and persona.

And that is no exaggeration. His character would not exist without his passion for his robe.

One night when wearing his entrance robe in the ring he was taking too much time folding it. This tested the patience of the crowd to near riotous atmosphere.

And when you're a heel, this is exactly what you want.

So, George Wagner ran with it. During his career he would enrage crowds across the country with his collection of over 100 robes decked out in lace, sequins, and fur.

Thousands of tickets and even thousands of televisions were sold with the goal to see Gorgeous George get his just deserves.

The entrance robe would become part of the abnormal norm that is professional wrestling.

Of course, when talking about entrance robes we must talk about "The Nature Boy" Ric Flair. The "stylin', profilin', limousine riding, jet flying, kiss-stealing, wheelin' and dealin', son of a gun" is the king of the entrance robe.

Since the 1970's, Ric Flair has graced the crowds with the awe-inspired customize-made garments of glory. These fabulous fabrics cost "The Man" a reportedly $10,000 a pop so they should definitely look great. And they most definitely Woo.

Ric Flair is known for many things. His great matches, his great promos, and his great entrance robes.

In 2008, the robe he wore at WrestleMania XXIV, was donated to, and was featured at the Smithsonian Institute in Washington D.C.

In 2017, one of Flair's iconic robes even sold for $27,000 in auction.

In the same year The Nature Boy was honored in the form of a beautiful statue. Of course, it's in an entrance robe.

Flair's contributions to professional wrestling are endless, but one that no one can argue is that he took the entrance robes to Space Mountain and beyond.

Some would attempt to rock the robe and fail to live up to its status.

Others would have success with the casual coat, some would go with the glitz, and a few would carry on legacies.

Whether it's for the majesty, the glamour, or the convenient warmth; a professional wrestling fan knows that the entrance robe should always be respected because we fans know that Ric Flair is always watching.

101 REASONS TO LOVE PRO WRESTLING

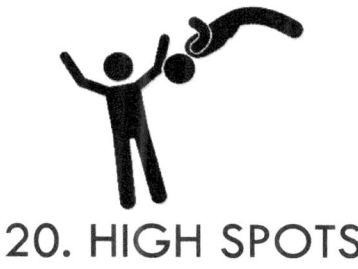

20. HIGH SPOTS

When spectating, there is nothing better than the rush of the big moment.

This boost of endorphins wakes up the crowd.

It's the big climax in music. In the NBA, it's a slam dunk. It's the Hail Mary pass. It's stealing home in the bottom of the ninth.

These moments are no stranger to professional wrestling.

However, the pioneering years of professional wrestling the landscape was a bit different from today.

Matches consisted of grappling and wear down holds as the wrestlers sought victory.

Leaving one's feet was unheard of unless it was done by the force of their opponent.

Then in the late 1920's, things began to change. The introduction of flying impact and risk-filled maneuvers were introduced. These big moves would be the groundwork of the high spot as we know it today.

Former NFL player Gus Sonnenberg would utilize the flying tackle.

Abe Coleman, the Hebrew Hercules; not to be confused with Abe Froman the "Sausage King of Chicago", is credited for the inclusion of the drop kick. Coleman claimed to have borrowed the idea from kangaroos.

Then Antonio Rocca adopted the dropkick, but also included hurricaranas and flying body presses.

The hurricarana itself was created by Huracan Ramirez, who would wrap his legs around his opponent's neck and roll them down.
Meanwhile in Mexico, Mando Guerrero was establishing the moonsault as

part of the lucha arsenal that already included many flips, dives, and leaps.

Then in the 1980's the idea of high flying and leaping moves became more of the norm. With some historic moments formed due to the high spot.

This would evolve in the 90's as wrestling's top stars became smaller and the risky moves became larger.

High flying legends like Rey Mysterio Jr, Ultimo Dragon, and a slew of others made a high-flying impact on a global scale.

By the turn of the century, the high spot became a standard in professional wrestling.

High spots are not always the flippity-do-dahs and top rope battles between the smaller weight classes. The bigger stars will leave their feet sometimes just as much as their lighter counterparts.

But yeah, a lot of today's high spots are still flippity-do-dahs.

Dives to the outside are in most matches.

Top rope moves have evolved into 450s, inverted 450s, and moves that leave the crowd in amazement and glee.

The risks have gone from simple rolls to rather uncomfortable results.

Our attention spans are shrinking, so keeping the attention of the crowd is a challenge. To keep up with this, more high spots are added.

And really, it has always been this way. Fans of grappling saw professional wrestling evolve into slams and power moves. Fans from the 80's saw smaller guys come in and literally flip the art of wrestling on its head.

Ultimately, professional wrestling matches tell a story.

If that story can be told with a big high spot or two it becomes that much more memorable... especially, if the opponent moves.

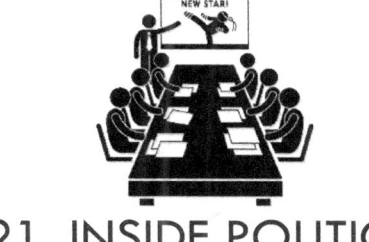

21. INSIDE POLITICS

Every culture, society, or organization has their own set of norms and rules that it is founded on.

Going back to even before the double crossing of Julius Cesar, there have always been scandals.

There is always a chain of command, a king of the jungle, and a lay of the land. With this comes controversy, inner-bickering, and internal battles.

Of course, there are governments and communities that have policies that are enforced by law.

But all cultures have their own regulatory scrutiny.

There are many examples of specific groups with specific rules.

In sports, its kangaroo courts deciding how to manage their team from within.

Be it a code of ethics, the code of the samurai, or the code of the mafia and street gangs, there are both spoken and unspoken rules.

Even your high school had a student council.

Every tribe has a chief.

In professional wrestling it's the promoter, the owner, or the respected veteran that guides the pulse of the locker room.

Professional wrestling has its own way of dealing with internal issues.

"The Montreal Screw Job" is the first thing that comes to mind.

101 REASONS TO LOVE PRO WRESTLING

Bret "The Hitman" Hart was leaving the company and did not want to drop the WWF Championship belt to "The Heartbreak Kid" Shawn Michaels in his home country of Canada.

The story then goes that Vince McMahon had no choice but to pull one over and essentially screw the Canadian hero.

This messy story is one of the biggest controversies in wrestling's long illustrious history. However, it is not the only story of this type.

There are plenty more cases of "locker room dirt".

In any form of collaborative art or team sports there are those who are unhappy with their role, their money, or their schedule.

This leads to wrestlers airing their dirty laundry about management.

When a wrestler needs money, attention, or a soap box to preach from they will work with random wrestling related production companies, podcasts, and websites to have revealing interviews about what goes or has gone on backstage.

These "shoot-style" interviews have blessed fans with a deep look behind the curtain.

And like Eric Bischoff proclaimed, "controversy sells."

The roar among the wrestling community rises when the juiciest of gossip, news, and interactions occur.

The cause and effect of these backstage antics have resulted in some of wrestling biggest events.

If Triple H had not been punished for taking part in the infamous "Curtain Call", a moment where real life friends broke kayfabe to hug goodbye in the ring, then "Stone Cold" Steve Austin would have never won the King of the Ring and cut his career-making 3:16 promo.

Then if "Stone Cold" Steve Austin hadn't shunned the idea of helping get Jeff Jarrett over then it's easy to wonder if he had ever left and started TNA Wrestling.

The same for Cody Rhodes. If he had been given more creative freedom and a better place on the card, would he have left and started All Elite Wrestling?

There are a whole lot of inside stories and lore about professional wrestling.

If it's not the murmurs of Hulk Hogan being hard to work with, then it's Dusty Rhodes holding people down when he was booking, or Booker T and Batista getting into a real fight while shooting a commercial.

Things have gotten out of hand like when Sid Vicious stabbed Arn Anderson with a pair of scissors or Enzo Amore being kicked out of the locker room or a million more of these little stories.

These types of shenanigans used to be settled behind closed doors and fans were lucky to hear a rumor.

Now wrestlers take to their social media to express themselves and their issues with wrestling management or their peers.

To someone on the outside, these tales can be quite tedious, but when you take on a passion in professional wrestling, you can't help but just eat it all up.

101 REASONS TO LOVE PRO WRESTLING

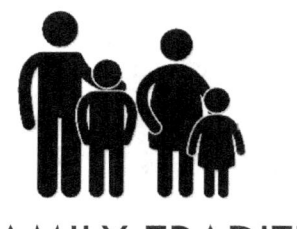

22. FAMILY TRADITION

A family is a group of people related either by birth, affinity, or co-residence.

This primal instinct maintains order and the overall well-being of society.

Families have their own rituals and traditions.

Some generations pass down heirlooms, some their secret family recipes, their passion for baseball, or even their love for professional wrestling.

Within the world of professional wrestling there are essentially four classes of families to be a part of.

You have your family at home.

It's the father, uncle, or grandmother that had their television set for the weekly matches or randomly took you to a local show.

With good child rearing, some of us are even fortunate enough to have wrestling in our lives before our first steps.

Even if a fan's family hates wrestling, there is a family built-in within the fan base itself. There are arenas with thousands and thousands of like-minded people who all are there for one thing... wrestling.

If we come across someone who follows wrestling in the real world, then it can open a world of possibilities.

When you speak the native language, it's a lot easier to feel at home.

There is also a family within the business.

The brothers and sisters who have graced the ring or experienced the backstage world are their own family.

101 REASONS TO LOVE PRO WRESTLING

It's been compared to the mafia. Through the shared passion, struggle, and respect for the industry, once a professional wrestler always a professional wrestler.

Like any family, there are fights, people who hate each other, cliques, and those who you'd rather not sit next to at the holiday table. Regardless, the camaraderie between those who make the magic for us is lifelong.

Then there are wrestling's first families.

These are the lineages of performers that have come from past generations of other performers.

The McMahon family has had multiple generations take the helm of control over the WWWF, WWF or WWE.

But it doesn't end there at all.

There are the Harts from Calgary. The Von Erichs from Texas. The Guerreros, the Ortons, the Rhodes, the Johnsons, the Flairs, the Funks, the Corinos and many more keeping their family names and legacies not just alive, but in the big of lights and engraved on championship belts.

A fan of wrestling knows these names and knows the stories of these living legacies. Professional wrestling as we know it would have a much different, and it's easy to say, "less fun" history without these fabled families doing their part.

Whether it's with blood, friends, peers, or a combination of the three, when you are a fan of wrestling you enjoy it, you absorb it, and you love it with kindred spirits.

The shared experience of a moment in professional wrestling is always best with family.

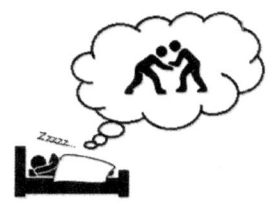

23. DREAM MATCHES

Who'd win in a fight? Batman or Superman?

Who'd win in an arm-wrestling contest? Tom Hanks or Bill Murray?

Who'd win in a cook-off? Gordon Ramsey or Julia Childs?

Who'd win in a dance off between Johnny Carson and Conan O'Brien?

How about a game of hopscotch between Pee-wee Herman and "Weird Al" Yankovic?

Maybe a cage fight between Judy Garland and Emma Stone?

A home run battle between Babe Ruth and Aaron Judge?

A boxing match between Muhammad Ali and Mike Tyson?

It goes on and on.

Hypothetical competition is a past time of anyone with a little bit of fandom and a whole lot of imagination.

The idea of dream matches in professional wrestling is nothing new.

There has always been fantasy warfare.

It's two performers matched-up due to the status of being the best. Other circumstances can make for a dream match like who is the best of a certain weight class, a certain era, a certain style of fighting.

The hefty task of living up to a dream match can quite daunting.

The anticipation that builds becomes an unmeasurable weight for the dream opponents to carry on their shoulders.

Tickets were sold, pay per views were ordered, programs, shirts, and merchandise were printed, and the tortuous wait is finally over.

Then there are two inevitable results of a dream match.

It will be magical. The match will electrify the crowd. The expectations are not only met but exceeded in spades. Our dreams come true, and we all go home and sleep like happy babies.

On the contrary, bad matches happen. The match falls flat. The crowd falls asleep or turns on the performers. Our dream match becomes a nightmare. And then the inevitable rematch, a recurring nightmare.

Then there are the dream matches that center around two iconic characters who never crossed paths due to being in different promotions. This was sadly the case with the Undertaker and Sting, who many still want to see go face to face.

Sometimes our dream matches just never happen. History misses the boat on giving us a desired battle. As the Thin White Duke so eloquently put it, 'Time may change me, But I can't trace time.'

Whatever the case, these never-going-to-happen dream matches will be forever craved and forever debated.

But that's what's great about professional wrestling. The next big dream match could always be right around the corner. But sadly, sometimes it's big match that got away.

It's not likely, but still possible to see a Rob Van Dam and Ricochet match to see who can fly the highest.

There wouldn't be too many fans upset if CM Punk got in the squared circle with the likes of an Adam Cole.

It's even more doubtful we'll ever get a Shawn Michaels versus AJ Styles to see who the best pure performer is.

We miss out on the battle of the icons of their eras in a "Stone Cold" Steve Austin and Hulk Hogan match.

Hayabusa vs. Shinsuke Nakamura, anyone?

Andre the Giant going monstrous toe to monstrous toe with Braun Strowman would have been fun.

Who'd have won between Daniel Bryan and Dusty Rhodes?

Or John Cena and the Ultimate Warrior?

How about Edge vs. Ricky "The Dragon" Steamboat, Triple H vs. Harley Race, or even Kofi Kingston vs. "Ravishing" Rick Rude?

Who wouldn't want to see Bret "The Hitman" Hart and Kurt Angle stretch each other for what would have been a technical clinic?

Would minds not be blown by a Ric Flair and Kenny Omega match?

The likelihood of a Steiner Brothers versus Usos tag team battle is incredibly slim.

And there is no chance we'll ever see the late great "Macho Man" Randy Savage take on Dolph Ziggler over the master of the elbow drop.

But like every dream match, it's definitely enjoyable to ponder the possibilities.

Dream on, professional wrestling fans, dream on...

101 REASONS TO LOVE PRO WRESTLING

24. MUSIC GIMMICKS

It is said that music is the universal language.

Anyone with two functioning ears can enjoy a great song.

With the passion for a great tune, there have always been an aura of celebrity around a great musician.

From the classical composers to the first big time rock stars.

Musicians have become celebrated figures for their talents and fame.

With the rise of character-based performers in professional wrestling during the 1970's and 1980's, it would have been silly for the industry to not adopt some of that rock star swagger.

There has been music in wrestling going back to the early days with characters like George Ringo, the wrestling Beatle, working in smaller Midwest territories.

But it would be Michael P.S. Hayze and the Freebirds to ignite the movement with their self-sung 80's blues rock "Badstreet USA".

Rock and roll would go on to forever have a couch to crash on in professional wrestling.

One of the best tag teams of all time were The Rock and Roll Express. In 1991, Van Hammer would represent that awkward time in between hair metal and grunge. Raven would take care of being a suitable front man for grunge rock in wrestling. The modern scene features the likes of Elias, who is actually quite the guitar player, carry the torch of rock and roll gimmicks.

In the 1980's we were also introduced to the Honky Tonk Man, a man in a jumpsuit with slick hair and swiveling hips. A character like this would be brushed off by many, but Wayne Ferris created a Hall of Fame career around the musical gimmick and as now is the longest reigning Intercontinental Champion of all time.

As music evolved, so did the music characters.

Hip Hop gimmicks would become a staple in the industry with the likes of PG13 showing up in the early 90's, Oscar from Men on a Mission dropping flows, New Jack's violent ring-work was a mirror to the violent gangsta rap of the time, then John Cena was rapping in the early 2000's all the way to one of the greatest careers of all time, and R-Truth rapping on the way to the ring for literally decades now.

With the Southern "Rasslin'" the concept of a country music gimmick would be often used. The mid-90's had Jeff Jarrett presenting himself as a country music singer from Nashville, Tennessee. Then we'd see The West Texas Rednecks team up as a country group that was not shy about their disdain for rap with the oh-so-wittily titled, "I Hate Rap" single. Then we would see a legit vocalist revealed in Mickie James "Hardcore Country" phase in TNA Wrestling.

At times, the music gimmicks reflect some of the more embarrassing times like Three Count, a three-man boy band in WCW made up of three very talented highflyers.

There have also been opera singers, misfits, KISS Demons, DJs, disco dancers, funk, punk, pop, and salsa.

Rock stars and legitimate musicians have their place in the ring as well. Chris Jericho's band Fozzy has had success, but he is not alone. Jimmy Hart, Jeff Hardy, Lita, Ron Killings, and others have released studio-recorded music.

The modern rock star lives their life on the road, entertaining thousands every night.

However, the life of a professional wrestler is a bit more tolling. The Rock star doesn't have to dodge flying folding chairs. But if you're Nickelback, a flying beer bottle is never off the table.

Australian rock icons AC/DC gave us, "For those about to rock, we salute you". But for those about to use rock as their gimmick...

We, the fan of professional wrestling, salute YOU.

101 REASONS TO LOVE PRO WRESTLING

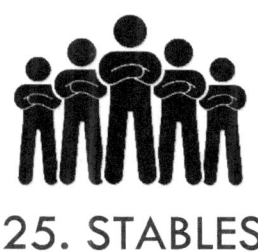

25. STABLES

Tribes go back to the dawn of time. It is a natural human instinct to join forces with those who are blood, in the same location, or even just like-minded.

Take this concept, add a little ultra-violence and you have a gang. As the movie "The Warriors" so poetically showcased, when you are on a journey back home you are bound to cross many turfs and some very eccentric gangs.

A professional wrestling fan taking a journey through their fandom are likely to tell you similar tales.

In the 1970's there was the First Family, the Heenan Family, the Dangerous Alliance, and others.

But in wrestling, the gangs are called "stables". In the world away from the ring, a stable would be used to describe a grouping of horses. In professional wrestling, there's only one group of horses that need to be discussed.

The Four Horsemen.

Formed in 1986, the Four Horsemen were one of the first big time groups of all time. They are also not just in the conversation for greatest stable of all time, they ARE the conversation.

The first incarnation featured "Nature Boy" Ric Flair, "The Enforcer" Arn Anderson, Ole Anderson, and Tully Blanchard with JJ Dillon as their manager. These men are all Hall of Famers on their own, but together they were easily the cream of the crop and unstoppable.

Then over the years, the men with four extended fingers would have some great members including Sting, Lex Luger, Brian Pillman, and more elite status wrestlers.

While there is no doubt on what the greatest stable of all time is, there are a few other legendary stables.

You have to include the New World Order in the discussion. The nWo was a group of Hall of Famers in their own right with Hulk Hogan, Scott Hall, Kevin Nash, Sean Waltman, and a handful of others.

For a few years during the 1990's this was the hottest thing in the business and had a gigantic amount of pop culture crossover.

But like most good things in wrestling, the nWo would eventually fizzle out.

Still, the impact of New World Order was made, and they will forever be part of history.

Then there is D-Generation X, another Hall of Fame stable. Started by "the Heartbreak Kid" Shawn Michaels, Hunter Hearst Helmsley, and the "Ninth Wonder of the World" Chyna.

With their crude and sophomoric humor, DX made their marks with crotch-chops and vulgar sayings. During the Attitude Era in the WWF, this was not only perfectly acceptable, but it was a huge success.

Shawn Michaels would leave due to injury, but Triple H added "X-Pac" Sean Waltman and the New Age Outlaws.

The group would last for several years and to this day, they are featured on special events.

The nWo and DX were not the only stables of the 1990's. There was the Dungeon of Doom, the Million Dollar Corporation, the Flock, the Nation of Domination, and it goes on and on.

The 2000's would see Evolution, Aces & Eights, The Embassy, and other's show up and represent the long lineage of wrestling stables.

Then in the 2010's, lightening was captured in a bottle when New Japan Pro Wrestling's Bullet Club hit the scene.

This stable had the likes of AJ Styles, Finn Balor, Adam Cole, Gallows, Anderson, and other global stars at one point.

Once the Young Bucks, Kenny Omega, Adam Page, and Cody Rhodes got on board the fans of independent and international wrestling ate it up.

These guys would eventually leave New Japan Pro Wrestling and start All Elite Wrestling, but the Bullet Club continues going into the 2020's.

It would be criminal to not mention NXT's best stable of all time and arguably the best stable of the late 2010's… The Undisputed Era.

Adam Cole, Roderick Strong, Bobby Fish, and Kyle O'Reilly showed a whole new generation of fans how to pull off a great group with style and absolutely no grace.

Then it would be remised to not mention the top stable of the 2020's in "The Bloodline" with Roman Reigns, the Usos, Paul Heyman, Solo Sika, and Sami Zayne.

There has also been a long tradition of three-man groups that have left a lasting impression. Going back to the Freebirds to Demolition to the Triple Threat to two of the most successful groups of all time, the New Day, and the Shield.

Stables are not always successful or as cool as the ones that have been mentioned. The Oddities, Los Boricuas, Kai En Tai, the Mean Street Posse, and Right to Censor are all forgettable or better forgotten.

To the outside world, gang warfare should never an acceptable solution.

However, in professional wrestling it is part of the past time and can be quite fun if done properly.

Whether you call a united group a stable, a cause, or a gang; a professional wrestler can accomplish quite a bit thanks to a well-formed collaboration of violence.

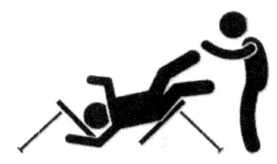

26. TABLE SPOTS

A folding table is a convenient piece of mobile furniture. It is a pretty simple, but necessary, design. A flat surface with foldable legs.

The origins of the folding table actually go back to ancient Egypt and would be utilized through the Colonial and Victorian eras.

The folding table would benefit from the mass production of the 20th century. In 1951 the folding table would be patented by Boris Cohen and Joseph Pucci. Thanks to Boris and Joseph, fans of professional wrestling were gifted another tool of choreographed torture.

The first time a folding table used in the history of the squared circle is debated. Some say tables were used as early as the 1940's. Others credit the 70's. Regardless, it is hard to imagine a street fight or crazy brawl not spilling into or on top of one of these pieces of convenient furniture.

In the late 70's, the gigantic Joe Leduc threw Jerry "The King" Lawler over the top rope and onto the announce table.

In 1984, Randy Savage pile drove Ricky Morton through a table in Memphis.

In 89, Terry Funk not only turned on him, but would pile drive "Nature Boy" Ric Flair on a table in the NWA. It did not break, but it added fire to their scorching rivalry.

In the WWF, the first notable table spot came during Saturday Night's Main Event in 1988 when "King" Harley Race laid Hulk Hogan on a ringside table and dove onto him. Not only did the Hulkster move, but the table did also not break.

Then seven years later, in 1995, the first WWF broken table spot happened when "Big Daddy Cool" Diesel knocked Canadian icon Bret "The Hitman" Hart off the ring apron and right through the ringside announcer's table.

From there it snowballed. The shock and awe of a destroyed table would evolve and become part of WWF and then the WWE's creative playbook.

When something is hardcore in North American wrestling, it can typically be traced back to Extreme Championship Wrestling.

A large part of the rise of table destruction can be credited to one man... the homicidal, the suicidal, and the genocidal Sabu! Sabu would use at least one table in just about all of his matches. Then the Dudley Boys would also adopt the table as a big part of their personas. When Bubba Ray Dudley shouts, "D-Von, get the table!" you knew what was coming... Exploding wood!

ECW would also have Public Enemy, Mike Awesome, and just about everyone else in ECW that broke tables as often as possible.

Of course, there's Mick Foley. Whether it's his death match start as Cactus Jack, his psychotic Mankind character, or even his groovy Dude Love the folding table has had an impact in his career as much as his great promos, cheap pops, and socks with drawn on faces.

WWE would have The Hardyz, Edge and Christian, and The Dudleys annihilate the wooden structures during the heyday of the TLC era.

It clearly did not end there. The art of rearranging furniture the hard way has become part of wrestling almost as much as a wristlock.

Whether it's set up as normal, rested in a corner, engulfed in flames, rested between the ring and guardrail, or however else a creative performer can come up with, the forceful demolition of a folding table always gets the fans on their feet.

Even if that means the ringside announcers have nowhere to rest their elbows.

27. THE LOOK AROUND HANDSHAKE

Wise men have made the eloquent proclamation that trust is something that is earned.

In life we are to trust our parents, authority, and the friends we have developed a legitimate bond with.

What happens when that trust is broken?

Would Judas had turned on Christ? Would Julius Caesar had been stabbed to death at the Theatre of Pompey? Would we still be calling traitors Benedict Arnold if in fact, Benedict Arnold didn't turn his back on America? Or would we even need a prison system at all if everyone followed the rules?

Betrayal runs rampant in a society of ruthless people looking out for themselves.

One gesture to cement the act of trust and goodwill is a firm handshake.

This symbolic act is no stranger to the culture of professional wrestling.

However, it's approached a bit differently than how "normal" society handles it...

Before another wrestler's extended hand is accepted a longtime troupe of the sport is to take a moment, absorb the situation, and slowly and exaggeratedly look around and outward to the live crowd to contemplate the situation.

Trusting just anyone is proven to be a foolish choice. The character of the performer offering said handshake must be evaluated.

This along with the reason the hand is being offered are factors that much be considered.

The shake is offered by a competitor after a long rivalry.

It could be after a great match.

A gesture of calling for a truce.

There is a plethora of reasons for the extended hand.

The handshake, whether you choose to accept, can lead to new journeys in one's career.

If the shake is not accepted, it is often a sign of a wrestler knowing better than to just throw their trust out there all willy-nilly.

Anyone who works in logic or experience can tell you that these handshakes don't often work out.

You might get attacked from behind, made a fool of, and left with egg and/or blood on your naive face.

Still... this is not always the case. Sometimes respect is respect. Sometimes the gesture is genuine. Sometimes you make a new friend.

But you never know.

History has proven that professional wrestling is a dog-eat-dog world and these performers all cursed with milk bone flavored under garments.

For years, this little gem has been part of professional wrestling. This is one of those little things that life-long fans come to just accept as perfectly normal.

Either you agree or do not agree that this tradition is one of the more fun aspects of wrestling so maybe we just should shake on it...

Or maybe not.

101 REASONS TO LOVE PRO WRESTLING

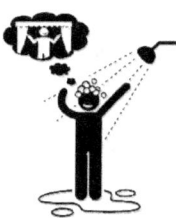

28. HYPOTHETICAL ENTRANCE MUSIC

When you're a fan of a sport or really any form of entertainment and you have any form of imagination it is hard not to picture yourself as part of it.

If you love superhero movies, it should be safe to assume one has thought of what superpower they would want.

If you are a fan of sports, it's easy to think of what jersey number you would want to wear.

We are all fans of something. We all have opinions. We all have a perception about who we are and what we represent.

This is true, even as fans of pro wrestling.

There is a vast library of interesting stories, odd-ball theories, and memorable facts that many professional wrestling fans share, debate, and react to.

We also take time to put ourselves in the shoes, or boots and kick pads, of the wrestlers we regularly watch.

An imaginative fan will consider all the possibilities of a situation...

Including our hypothetical entrance music.

If you ever utilized a "create-a-wrestler" feature in a video game, attempted backyard wrestling, or had an epiphany while sitting in traffic or during a morning shower then it is very likely you know exactly what song you would come in through the entrance curtains with.

Sometimes it just happens out of nowhere. You'll be out and about and hear the opening guitar riff or the contagious beat of a song you've heard a million times and start to visualize the "break" to enter to think how it would be awesome for a made-up character, yourself, or even as an alternative choice to a favorite on TV.

There are a copious factors to ponder when pondering.

What kind of character do you want to portray? If you are into hip hop, odds are your music will be hip hop. If you want to be a dark and spooky character, then your music would be dark and spooky.

What kind of energy do you want to create? Do you want to get the crowd pumped? Do you want to shock them? Is your plan to create a grand entrance similar to a "Nature Boy" Ric Flair or "Macho Man" Randy Savage then maybe a classical tune is right for you.

Then, what is your favorite band? Your favorite song? What gets you pumped? What would get you in the right frame of mind to enter the ring and perform at your best?

While a wrestler on television might not always have the option to what they come out to due to the creative management having differing opinions or an outrageous rights fee that the company refuses to shell out for, you do NOT have this dilemma. In a hypothetical world, the possibilities are endless.

So, let's break this down.

When YOU hear the announcer shout, "Now, coming to the ring... From wherever you are... Weighting in at whatever you weight and standing at however tall you are..." what hypothetical entrance music comes to YOUR mind?

What else are you going to play when you hold up your replica championship belt in the mirror?

101 REASONS TO LOVE PRO WRESTLING

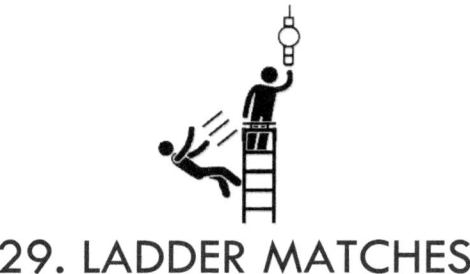

29. LADDER MATCHES

A ladder is a structure, a piece of equipment, that consists of horizontal steps placed in between two vertical supports. Its purpose is to reach elevated areas and is a standard tool for firemen, painters, and even swimmers looking to exit a pool.

There is also the metaphor that is often used about our working careers is climbing the ladder of success.

While this is absolutely true in professional wrestling, it's not always just a metaphor.

You literally must climb the ladder of success.

Then when you're up there, you have to retrieve a dangling championship belt.

This is a Ladder Match.

A championship belt, or a briefcase, or really any object is hung from the ceiling. Then the competitors of the match have one objective, get it down.

And the only way to achieve this goal is to use a company provided ladder.

When clawing and climbing this ladder of success, anything goes. If you want to win this specialty match, you should be prepared for pain.

If there is already a ladder present and anything goes, it is easy to imagine the pending carnage.

The wrestlers use the ladder as a weapon.

You can slam someone on it, smash them between it, swing it in pursuit of knocking them down, or even leap off it on to your opponent to add to the splendid spectacle that is a Ladder Match.

The evolution of this match has led to some of the most creative spots and visuals wrestling has seen.

The origins of the Ladder Match go back to the early 1970's. Canada's Stampede Wrestling would feature the first ever of its kind when Dan Kroffat and Tor Kamata were climbing for a wad of money.

In 1987, the British-based World of Sport would showcase a "disco challenge" Ladder Match where Kendo Nagasaki and Clive Myers would use a ladder to reach a gold disco record.

The Stu Hart-owned Stampede Wrestling would also have a Ladder Match in 1983 that saw Bret Hart take on Bad New Allen.

Bret Hart took the idea with him to the World Wrestling Federation, where he and Shawn Michaels would climb and fight for the Intercontinental Title Belt.

The Ladder Match would reach new heights in 1994 when "The Bad Guy" Razor Ramon would defeat "The Heartbreak Kid" Shawn Michaels at WrestleMania 10.

This match not only brought the Ladder Match to the mainstream, but it set the bar very high.

So high that not many one-on-one Ladder Matches today come close to its impact or enjoyment.

There would be a remarkable rematch a year later with Michaels winning.

The Rock and Triple H tearing it down at Summer Slam in 1998, and then the Hardyz battling it out with Edge and Christian in 1999 to reach a bag of cash.

That tag team match would open the doors to what many fans are accustomed to today. With the inclusion of The Dudley Boyz, the Hardyz, and Edge and Christian would unleash the TLC phenomenon. That's Tables, Ladders, and Chairs.

Since then, outside of 2013, there have been at least one Ladder Match a year in the WWE with many years having a handful.

They still have Ladder Matches from time to time, but you can for sure count on the annual Money in the Bank matches that see multiple competitors' claw, climb, and crush each other in their journey towards reaching the Money in the Bank briefcase. A symbolic briefcase that grants the winner a title shot on the demand.

It's not just the WWE. World Championship Wrestling had Ladder Matches going back to 1987 when Dusty Rhodes took on Tully Blanchard in a Barbed Wire Ladder Match with the prize of $100,000 hanging from the ceiling.

Ten years later the likes of Eddie Guerrero vs. "Syxx" Sean Waltman would battle for the United States Title, Goldberg and Scott Hall reaching for a Taser, the Jung Dragons and 3 Count going after a record contract, and more.

Extreme Championship Wrestling gave us Stairway to Hell Ladder Matches, Impact Wrestling had theirs with the Ultimate X twist, Ring of Honor put out some great Ladder Wars, and the Ladder Match has already been a part of All Elite Wrestling's early run.

As with anything, times change, and things evolve. The modern Ladder Match can have more and more competitors added, more and more ladders added to the war, more and more stipulations, and more and more creativity unveiled.

But some traditions are just always going to be part of the match by design.

Call it a cliche or a tired act, but the "slow climb" is never going away.

This is when someone climbs slower than a deceased turtle up the ladder for suspenseful purposes.

Rung by rung the wrestler ascends towards the belt.

The anticipation builds, the wrestler reaches, and then it's simple; they get knocked off or they inevitably retrieve the prize and victory.

Silly? Of course. But you just have to accept it as "wrestling being wrestling" and there is nothing wrong with that.

You might not always get a classic like Razor and Shawn, but a Ladder Match is a lot like the pizza of professional wrestling.

Even when it's bad, it's still pretty awesome.

30. HEEL TURNS

Sometimes good people go bad.

Everyone wants to be the hero of their own story, but sometimes one has nowhere else to turn but evil.

An individual's moral compass can take them in various directions.

Sometimes that direction is just bad.

It's a sad reality, but there are copious amounts of examples of this throughout written history.

We're talking about Michael Corleone going bad and embracing his new role as "The Godfather".

Harvey Dent going from a pillar of the Gotham community to a full-fledged monster as Two-Face.

Sometimes people just get pushed too far and go off the deep end like Travis Bickle in "Taxi Driver" or Jack Torrance in "The Shining" or Walter White in "Breaking Bad".

It could also just be the character's fate as in Anakin Skywalker becoming Darth Vader.

The villain rises with an angry edge, a chip on their shoulder, and a goal of destroying the hero.

When friend ships sail there is always a chance of being thrown overboard or sinking.

Of course, this is a long-time tradition in the world that is professional wrestling.

Everyone loves a good guy in wrestling. He has done good, he tries hard, he is of good moral character, and he is going to do his best to make sure YOU, the fan, goes home happy.

Then, out of nowhere, they just snap!

They beat up another good guy, they let their "real emotions" be known, or they just flat out change their character and motives.

It's that big turning point in a character arch that gives everyone a chance to refresh and try something new.

There have been many memorable and historic heel turns in professional wrestling.

In the 1980's "The Immortal" Hulk Hogan was as face as you could get. Because of this it was very easy for the company to create new bad guys just by having them turn on the Hulkster. This could include the likes of Andre the Giant being tired of Hogan's long reign as champion. "Macho Man" Randy Savage turning in a jealous rage. Paul Orndorff would reveal his heel turn on Hogan by joining the Heenan Family. And even Tugboat turned on Hogan to become Typhoon of the Natural Disasters.

Then in the late 90's, Hogan would return the favor by breaking the hearts of his fans as he turned on them and WCW. In what many consider the biggest heel turn of all time, this event would lead to the creation of his heel "Hollywood" Hogan persona.

Families have seen heel turns as well. Owen Hart's vicious attack on his older brother Bret's leg laid the groundwork for Owen's rise up the card.

The Hardy Boyz have seen their share of drama as well.

This proves that while blood might be thicker than water, it is definitely not thicker than gold.

Tag teams rarely last forever.

This sentiment was in full display when Shawn Michaels threw Marty Jannetty through a window in a moment that has gone down in history as one of the more famous betrayals.

It's not just Hogan, family squabbles, and broken tag teams. Sometimes the heartbreak of a heel turn is just a shocking occurrence.

There are still fans with PTSD over the times "Stone Cold" Steve Austin and The Rock sold their souls to align with the evil "Mr. McMahon".

Mentor Bruno Sammartino never expected his protege Larry Zbyszko to turn and no one would have ever imagined Paul Bearer turning on The Undertaker.

That is just a few of the more vile and unexpected turns in wrestling.

There are many more in the past and many more to come in the future.

Wherever there is a hero, there is someone waiting to stab them in the back.

So, if you ever find yourself feeling like a hero in your own story beware.

Because as "Stone Cold" Steve Austin put it, D.T.A…

Don't Trust Anyone.

Especially… Austin.

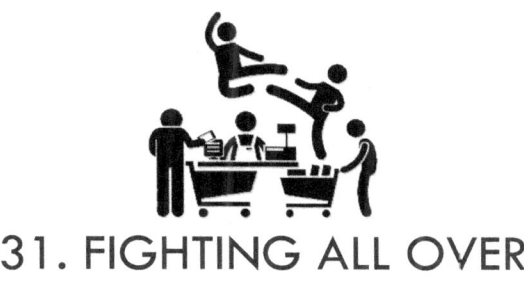

31. FIGHTING ALL OVER

Not all wars are fought on the battlefield.

It is not uncommon for a fight to not be in a structured environment.

We know wrestling excels in the four-sided ring.

It's a standard that needs to remain for pro wrestling to, quite frankly, be pro wrestling.

Without the four-sided ring it's merely a badly acted action movie.

Still, it is hard not to love the well-built matches and rivalries go that extra distance.

In instances like these, it is not unheard of for a fight to end up or even start outside of the ring.

The "Falls Count Anywhere" match makes the notion fighting outside of the confines of the ring into an actual match stipulation.

The roots of this match type go back to at least the 70's, but there is much debate about the first of its kind.

However, in the mid-1900's, there were performers like Bruiser Brody that would have wild brawls that would spill out to the ringside area.

As soon as the televised approach to professional wrestling came into play, there has always been a fair share of backstage attacks that left rivals laying.

This story-arch building contraption is now a commonality of the presentation. In the modern landscape of wrestling, performers almost always take their fight at ringside.

But over the years, it is not uncommon to see a fight in the crowd, in the stands, on the entrance ramp or in random hallways.

Fighting all over peaked on the mainstream level and was very common when WWF had the "Hardcore Title" where fights would go into random locations like outside the arena, in lakes, in bars, or even parking lots.

In the late 1980's, Antonio Inoki and Masa Saito's crazy rivalry was capped off with a crazy match concept.

The two would square off in an "Island Death Match". A match where the two battled for over two hours on a legendary deserted island.

In March of 1995, WCW's Uncensored Pay Per View featured a "King of the Road" match between Dustin Runnels and Blacktop Bully in the back of a moving vehicle.

Then at Summer Slam in 1996, the WWF saw The Undertaker take on Mankind in the iconic Boiler Room Brawl that started in the boiler room and went all throughout the backstage area on their way to the ring.

There have been Hollywood Backlot Brawls, Empty Arena Matches, and Final Deletions. There are many more examples of scrapping in obscure scenery, but one very entertaining instance stands out to most longtime fans.

In December of 2001, the concept of brawling in obscure locations was taken to the next level. On a very memorable episode of Smackdown, Booker T and "Stone Cold" Steve Austin would brawl it out in a California grocery store. Yes, a grocery store.

The two battled all over the store giving the fans a true "blue light special", while giving the clerks a bit to clean up on aisle... well, all of the aisles.

Every match doesn't need to be settled in this manner. A great match inside the ring is always what will garner the most for the art form.

But a great brawl is always going to be a great brawl no matter where it is.

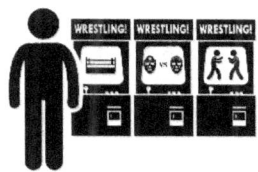

32. THE VIDEO GAMES

Video games go back all the way to the 1950's when computer scientists would design simple games and simulations for fun.

However, video games would not hit the mainstream until the 1970's and 80's when arcade games started to hit the scene.

These coin-operated machines became popular attractions at malls and would engage the youth with digital spectacle.

Of course, with anything new in pop culture, professional wrestling would take a part in it.

The first major arcade release was "Tag Team Wrestling", also known as "The Big Pro Wrestling". Released in 1983 by Technos, a company best known for the iconic "Double Dragon".

There would eventually be other arcade games under the professional wrestling umbrella, but when the personal consoles came into play the world of video games would never be the same.

In 1987 WWF's "MicroLeague Wrestling" would enter the scene for Commodore 64 and one of the early versions of Atari. The first WWF home console game would tout that it features exclusive digitized video action.

What this means was they had a list of moves to choose from and base on what you'd select a very low-resolution image would appear.

This sounds as exciting as picking a paint color from a list and watching it dry... digitally.

Then things got a bit better, 8-bit better, to be exact.

101 REASONS TO LOVE PRO WRESTLING

With the introduction of the Nintendo Entertainment System, we could now have actual matches in the comfort of our own homes. This would start with 1989's WWF "WrestleMania".

Choosing from Hulk Hogan, Andre the Giant, "Macho Man" Randy Savage, "The Million Dollar Man" Ted DeBiase, Bam Bam Bigelow, and The Honky Tonk Man, players would fight through the roster on their way to hopefully becoming the WWF Champion.

That same year, WCW Wrestling was released with their own roster of wrestlers with the same objective of becoming the champ.

Similar games would pop up every year or two.

The likes of WWF "WrestleMania Challenge" and others would have minor updates on game play and a few different wrestlers added here and there but ultimately the arcade games were still the best experiences.

This would include WWF "Superstars" in 1989 and 1991's WWF "WrestleFest". "WrestleFest" would be considered one of the most popular and beloved wrestling games of all time. The roster was expanded from the WWF "Superstars" edition, but also more selectable match modes. Players could pick from the normal one-on-one matches, tag team matches, and the Royal Rumble mode that would feature a very entertaining battle royal.

When the 16-bit Super Nintendo was released, more wrestling was to follow.

"Super WrestleMania" was released in 1992. This game gave us the same match modes as prior releases but gave players the coveted Survivor Series four-on-four elimination matches to enjoy.

Other 16-bit SNES games would include 1993's "Royal Rumble" and then 1994's WWF "Raw".

These wouldn't be the only wrestling games for Super Nintendo. WCW had "Super Brawl Wrestling", New Japan Pro-Wrestling had "Chou Senshi in Tokyo Dome", there was the first Fire Pro game: "Fire Pro Women: All-Star Dream Slam", and a few different All Japan Pro Wrestling games to name a couple.

There would be other games sprinkled in for other platforms like WWF "Rage in the Cage" for Sega CD, "King of the Ring" for Game Boy, and other forgettable cartridge-based competition.

PlayStation then entered the scene and life as we wrestling game fans knew it would be forever changed.

In 1995 Acclaim released WWF "WrestleMania: The Arcade Game". This game was ridiculous. The characters looked much better than the older games, but the gameplay was closer to an "NBA Jam" or "Mortal Kombat".

We're talking nonsense like Razor Ramon's arms transform into literal razors and Doink the Clown using a mallet that would manifest out of thin air.

Yeah, this was amusing... but bad.

Acclaim would follow this up with WWF "In Your House".

Same nonsense, just more nonsense-ier.

In 1998, things got back to normal with WWF "War Zone". Released on PlayStation and Nintendo 64, this game had cage matches, the Royal Rumble, tornado tag, and now Hardcore.

"War Zone" featured 18 wrestlers, but most notably a Create-A-Wrestler mode that allowed the player to make up a new character or attempt to recreate their favorites who were not included in the playable roster.

Acclaim followed this up with WWF "Attitude". It was an updated version of "War Zone" that had more characters as well as the inclusion of the First Blood and I Quit Matches.

WCW would unleash "WCW vs. The World" and "WCW vs. nWo: World Tour". Two games that had a more mature grappling system with a large array of characters. Many were WCW mainstays, but also huge stars from the world with made-up names to avoid any legal ramifications.

In 1999, one of the most popular releases was WWF "WrestleMania 2000" for Nintendo 64. A game that had most of what was seen in games before but with one of the most beloved game engines of all time.

In 2000, WWF teamed with THQ for WWF "Smackdown!"

This would be the first of many to hit the shelves in the early 2000's. Story mode was a huge hit as players would be able to experience the life of a wrestler with backstage antics, feuds, and goals of becoming champion.

The "Smackdown" series would see many releases going into 2011. Each with their own updates, quirks, and fun. They would go from PlayStation to PlayStation 2 and 3 as fans across the globe battled it out in a digital world of animated violence.

Then the "WWE 2K" series arrived. Just as there "Madden" football games seeing new releases launched every year, the 2K games had consistent updates.

The 2K platforms would always reflect the times. If a new gaming system was released, they'd be right on board with it. This meant we'd go from PlayStation 2 to PlayStation 3, Nintendo's Wii, and Xbox 360. From there the next wave with PlayStation 4 and Xbox One.

As time went on, the games got a little better and then a lot better.

People can nitpick, but these games have always been fairly consistent in terms of fun and popularity.

Over the years there has been "Fire Pro Wrestling", ECW games, TNA games, and a slew of other random, but beloved in their own right, wrestling video games.

Some say it's a good create-a-wrestler, some love the season mode, or even the entrances and arena variety but professional wrestling games are here to stay as long as both video games and professional wrestling exist.

Just like how vinyl has made a comeback, what was old has become new again.

In 2019, game developer Retrosoft Studios announced that a sequel to the old WWF "WrestleFest" game was in the works. "RetroMania Wrestling" brought the old school appeal of simpler times back with a game full of legends and independent stars not under contract to the major companies.

The buzz around the release has been great to say the least.

This would also be the case with the first All Elite Wrestling game.

If you're a fan of wrestling who wouldn't want to select their favorite wrestler and square off against a friend in a battle of button smashing and occasionally legitimate skill?

Ultimately, they are just video games, so it's mostly a fun waste of time.

At least with this waste of time, bragging rights are to be gained.

101 REASONS TO LOVE PRO WRESTLING

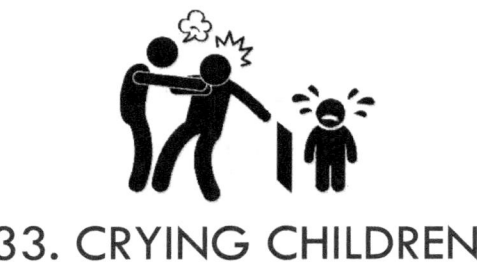

33. CRYING CHILDREN

Crying is part of our natural make-up.

It's a nonverbal communication of distress that often occurs the moment we are released from the womb.

The endocrine system is triggered to release hormones to the ocular area.

Translation: Things make us cry.

Physical and mental strength has no baring in this. Everyone cries. Whether it's physical pain, emotional distress, an overabundance of elation, or something internal that can't be described.

For the most part, the reasons for crying are fairly obvious and we should know and understand them. We are personally affected by something, and our body reacts.

Sometimes people are emotionally impacted by the arts. A masterful painting, a soul-wrenching song, or an extremely engaging movie will strike an internal chord that results in a teary-eyed surprise.

In the movie, "A League of Their Own", Tom Hanks declares "There's no crying in baseball".

However, there is definitely crying in professional wrestling.

Longtime fans of wrestling have seen this occurrence on numerous occasions.

There's the typical moment when a bad guy upsets the children in the crowd to the point of drawing tears from their little faces.

In the same respect, a child will be overcome with happiness when their hero finally overcomes the obstacles.

But it does not end there. There are numerous moments when a fan will be overwhelmed with emotion.

Emotions are a wild uncontrollable beast.

We grow old and become jaded people.

However, when those involved with professional wrestling do their jobs right, they can manipulate the mightiest of people.

It happens when a performer finally reaches their goals.

It happens when one of our favorites is forced to hang it up and call it a career.

It happens when a hero passes away.

It happens when we see someone struggle through adversity only to become injured and taken out.

It happens when we are impacted by the story of true love.

We fans tear up, weep, or in the least whimper at the presentation in front of us.

That's the magic.

Just like the masterful painting, the soul-wrenching song, or the extremely engaging movie, we are deeply moved by the story or invested in the careers of the performers we watch week in and week out, professional wrestling brings out our inner child.

You have to honestly ask yourself, if you've never felt yourself overwhelmed with emotion while following wrestling then are you even a real fan of professional wrestling at all?

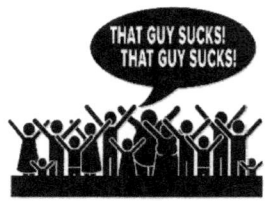

34. CROWD CHANTS

For as long as humans have gathered there have been an exhibition of herd mentality.

The conception of chanting crowds traces back to the dawn of man.

There are chants against political figures, sacred Gregorian chants, or other religious recitations, and chants of warriors preparing, entering, or leaving battle.

The historic utilization of chants goes on and on. One of the most appreciated and long-term venues for crowd chants is athletic competition.

Spanish crowds chant "ole" towards bullfighting.

English football fans have their own organized salutes as well.

There is the Tomahawk Chop still used by the fans of the Atlanta Braves baseball them for some reason.

Then there is a whole collection of crowd chants inspired by the ever-so creative and passionate fans of professional wrestling that have shown up in other sports.

Vulgar chants like "A-Hole" or "B.S." or the musical "Na Na Na Hey Hey Hey Goodbye", and a variety of others have begun in wrestling and then found their way into other sporting event crowds.

Professional wrestling has proven that virtually anything can be a chant if it has an organized cadence.

It's electricity and interactive camaraderie that create these moments.

If there was a foreign wrestler taking on an American, the chants of "U-S-A" would overtake the arena.

The crowds of Extreme Championship Wrestling were just as extreme as the performers. The company has been gone for a long time, but when something hardcore goes down the chant of "E-C-W" is always on the tips of the tongues of the fans resting on the edges of their seats.

In the mid-1990's it was never unheard of to hear the crowd chant "you f'd up", "f' him up Taz-f' him up", and even the now embarrassing chants of "she's a crack whore".

These are just a few, but there were others just as vulgar and some you'd be mortified to even ponder, that alone chant along with a crowd.

But there is a whole song book full of great chants outside of the standard boos and cheers.

Over the years, wrestling fans have chanted along with the catch phrases of their chosen heroes.

We scream "Yes! Yes! Yes!" in unison whenever Daniel Bryan raises his two index fingers over and over.

We "Wooo" along with the "Nature Boy" Ric Flair.

We will even sing-along with entrance music, whether there's words or not.

There are dueling chants where the crowd is split on who they want to succeed or their collective opinion of a specific wrestler.

We hear and shout "this is awesome" when the crowd appreciated what is in front of them.

There's always a chance of a "boring" chant when the crowd feels under whelmed.

On the contrary, a crowd will not by shy with a thrilling "fight-for-ever" chant in the midst of an extraordinary match.

Then when there is respect for a new champion a "you deserve it" chant is not uncommon.

If someone is retiring, we chant "please don't go" or "thank you" towards the exiting performer.

If someone makes a comeback to the squared circle a "welcome back" chant can be called for.

Or it could be the mere absence of a fan favorite, like Ric Flair in 1991 WCW, that brings out a "we want Flair" from the masses.

Maybe the rapid fans are so in love with someone delivering a big move that they request more with a "one more time" chant.

When the crowd sees a performer taking a big risk the chant of "please don't die" can add to the moment.

There is even a "you still got it" chant ready be unleashed whenever an old timer shows off their lingering skill set.

If it can be chanted, the fans of professional wrestling will always find a way.

If you ever find yourself in arenas for other sports you will most likely enjoy the experience, but when it comes down to it, a hundred wrestling fans chanting and popping is much cooler than even 20,000 fans waiting for something to finally happen at a hockey game or baseball game.

35. GIMMICK MATCHES

Once we start enjoying something it is always inevitable for a little extra to be added to keep us coming back for more.

In the 90's, moviegoers would love a movie and see it multiple times in the theatre, but once the DVD came out it would always include bonus scenes, directors' commentary, and additional perks.

Ice cream is delicious, but the extra whipped cream and cherry on top add a lot more excitement to the dish.

Broadcast television was once the talk of the town, but cable companies came in and added extra channels to keep the viewing consumer happy.

Bakers could sell a dozen donuts based on the deliciousness of the sugary pasty treat, but a baker's dozen gave us that extra donut to indulge in.

It is in our nature to want more, despite how much we already appreciate something.

Professional wrestling is no different.

People who love professional wrestling love professional wrestling matches.

But sometimes, a special match adds flavor to the already delectable dish.

These specialty matches are essentially gimmick matches. A gimmick is exploited to sell, and these matches definitely accomplish this goal.

In the earlier days of professional wrestling, a gimmick match would be included into the match-making mix much differently than what we see today.

The old mentality was when a long-term feud got so heated, they had no choice but to put the two fighters in a special match to inflict more pain for the enjoyment of the paying crowd.

The classics are Street Fights, Cage Matches, Falls Count Anywhere, 2 Out Of 3, or even a Strap Match.

Basically, it's anything that's not a standard good ol' fashion "one on one" competition.

Later on, wrestling would include Ladder Matches, Battle Royals, and even Death Matches.

As time evolved, so did the creativity.

The WWE would introduce Hell in A Cell, Tables, Ladders, and Chairs matches, Money in the Bank, Elimination Chambers, and a slew of other gimmick matches in attempt to draw larger crowds and larger viewing audiences.

Then there is the flip side of a gimmick match, one just being added for fun.

In the past we'd see a First Blood Match or something just as devastating to settle a long rivalry, but now they include a gimmick match just to include one.

There is an abundance of gimmick matches being used today without much rhyme or reason.

Ladder Matches are seen in many promotions.

As are Cage Matches, No Holds Barred, and many of the classics. However, WWE has taken it a step further with their presentation of gimmick matches.

Of course, the classic Royal Rumble match is always a favorite, but they've also included Pay Per Views specifically promoting annual gimmick matches in the "Elimination Chamber" and "TLC".

The gimmick match was once a specialty and something unexpected that would be announced to add fuel to an already burning fire.

In current times, they occur for no reason and casually happen when the calendar calls for it.

Regardless, a great gimmick match can still always be that extra whipped cream and cherry on top.

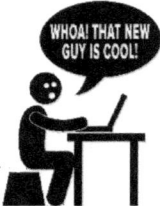

36. DISCOVERING NEW TALENT

There is a natural desire to be one step ahead of the curve.

Everyone yearns to be on the cutting edge of everything.

People flock to long lines to have access to modern technology.

Those on the stock market invest based on the economic futures.

Similarly, this is something everyone on all levels of fandom can appreciate.

The world of professional wrestling is the same in many ways, especially when it comes to discovering new talent.

Fans of mainstream wrestling on television, who don't follow the independent promotions, miss out on the evolution of someone's career on their way to debuting on television. These fans are exposed to new talent through vignettes and debuts and get to form their own conclusion if someone will be a "Blue Chipper" or not.

In the pre-technology eras, the only real way to see someone outside of your local territory was through tape trading with other fans, reading magazines, or simply through word of mouth.

Now it's much easier to follow a wrestler's journey.

We have access to companies who stream their shows, random You Tube matches, wrestling websites, and various other ways to absorb what is going on both nationally and internationally.

This is an investment of time. We see someone gain momentum in the smaller companies and work their way up the ladder towards their goal of world-wide exposure.

Independent fans of old were able to see the young up and comers like CM Punk and Colt Cabana work the circuit before landing in Ring of Honor and then beyond.

Likewise, fans have seen the likes of Daniel Bryan evolve from "The American Dragon" Brian Danielson to a multi-time World Champion in the WWE and back again in AEW.

Fans have witnessed the likes of Teddy Hart gain momentum and then their stock plummets for various reasons and never make it to a larger spotlight.

However, most only saw Hall of Famers like The Rock grow from their modest WWF debuts with characters like Rocky Maivia and later become the most electrifying entertainer of all time.

These folks missed out on his teeth-cutting phase as Flex Cavanna.

Sometimes we have the opportunity to see someone like a Rob Van Dam rise through the ranks of ECW before landing in the WWF. ECW fans already knew he was the "whole fn' show", but it would take WWF fans a little longer to come up with the same conclusion.

The WWE has recognized the phenomenon of following one's odyssey to the top and has turned their developmental league, NXT, into one of the most exciting shows in the current landscape of the sport.

On the contrary, sometimes a big fish in a small pond flounder in the bigger companies. Like any investment, not all will pan out. Not all will find their place on the big show.

Even if you follow an indie performer from ring crew to World Title status or if you follow someone from WWE vignette to World Title, discovering new talent is an enthralling subsidized venture.

It's just always cool to legitimately be able to say you were a fan of someone "from the start".

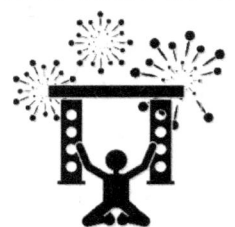

37. GRAND ENTRANCES

The Queen of England, the United States President, and professional wrestlers all have many things in common.

They have a large presence, take control of the room, and when they enter a room people stop in their steps and pay attention.

This is just a commonality of the nature of their characters.

In the WWE sense, an entrance is vital. There are fireworks, videos, lights, loud music, and as much glitz and glamour of any given Superbowl Halftime Show. That's just a normal weekly RAW or Smackdown.

WCW had the cool tunnels that Impact Wrestling and later All Elite Wrestling would eventually copy for their first few years.

The simple brick wall entrance that ECW would use for years has been duplicated in a million independent wrestling shows and is still out there in full force.

However, there are times a grand entrance is necessary for the bigger matches and events.

At WrestleMania the entrance stage is so elaborate and grand that it rivals ANY live entertainment production out there. It's a spectacle in the pure sensation of the word.

WrestleMania 3 had mini-ring carts carry the wrestlers to the ring. WrestleMania 12 saw Shawn Michaels ride a zip-line from the entrance to the ring. Then in many WrestleMania's the wrestler's entrance music would be performed live by the actual band.

While there are many grand entrances from the history of WrestleMania, it doesn't end there.

The Shield would enter through the crowd.

NXT has had their share of great live performances and elaborate entrances prior to the big fights.

Vehicles aren't out of the question. Legion of Doom came to the ring riding motorcycles at Summer Slam 92. D-Generation X entered with a tank at Summer Slam 2009.

The Undertaker's entrance alone is magic, but he has had some of the grandest entrances of all time.

These amazing walks to the ring are not exclusive to Vince McMahon's company.

Sting used to drop down from the rafters in WCW.

New Jack's theme of "Natural Born Killers" would blare through the speakers as he ran out armed with a slew of weapons to beat people up. The Ice Cube and Dr. Dre song would boom from the speakers the entire duration of the bedlam.

New Japan Pro Wrestling would highlight their biggest show of the year with awe-inspiring entrances.

When there is a big fight, there are a lot of features that go into the big fight feel.

In 2020, fans of boxing saw Fury and Wilder make grand entrances, but it is pretty safe to say where this inspiration came from.

If someone has watched the highly creative art form for long enough, they will surely have their own favorites from the long illustrious lineage of wrestling.

101 REASONS TO LOVE PRO WRESTLING

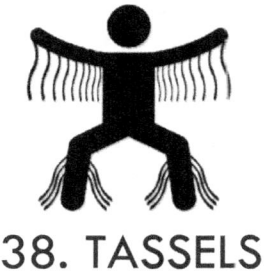

38. TASSELS

Fancy and glammed-up clothing is nothing new at all.

Elaborate garb has been part of history for many centuries.

One of the featured pieces of this are tassels.

Yes, tassels.

Tassels are a decorative finishing feature found on many clothing options from the past and present.

Tassels are in the bible, they were worn by kings and queens, and have been included in many military uniforms.

While some of these ancient outlets for tassels are still in existence, unless you're in the circus, the theatre, or gymnastics there aren't many opportunities to wear tassels.

That is, unless you're a professional wrestler.

Be it on their jacket, arms, or their boots, it's always a fun visual to see someone flying around with a little extra flair.

Tassels were a popular part of people's gear in the 1970's and 80's.

If you watched wrestling during this time frame, it would be hard to not see the stripped fabric phenomenon.

The Rock and Roll Express, The Rockers, The British Bulldog, "Macho Man" Randy Savage, and many others rocked the tassels.

The Ultimate Warrior was an iconic wrestling figure known for his face make-up and being a wild persona, but would his famous rope shake had been as cool without the ruffling of his tassels? Probably not.

As time went on, the utilization of tassels faded out.

Sure, there was the likes of "The Franchise" Shane Douglas wearing them on his boots, but the late 90's and early 2000's saw a tassel drought.

In more recent years, they've been popping back up.

The Young Bucks have a retro look that encompasses the fun of tassels.

They haven't completely gone away outside of super kick parties.

Bayley's amazing NXT face run saw tassels again at the top of the card.

Tyler Breeze, Paul London, and others in the current millennium have also had fun with the fringe.

Just like the hair flying in the air for a big move or sell, the tassel is another little dramatic visual that adds to the performance.

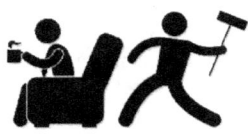

39. TRYING IT AT HOME

Idolization is nothing out of the norm.

Everyone wants to be like their heroes.

There aren't many playground sport games that don't involve at least one kid in the jersey of their favorite player.

Gatorade made an entire marketing campaign based around people wanting to be like Michael Jordan.

This was the "I Wanna Be Like Mike" commercials, that aired a ton during the 90's.

In the same vein, we toss up jump shots and imagine we're making a shot in the NBA like our favorite players.

However, when you're a fan of the choreographed violence that is professional wrestling, we have been told for years, "Don't Try This at Home".

Wrestling companies don't want the lawsuits of being a bad influence, but let's be realistic here... we definitely try it at home.

In reality, no one should be attempting the big moves we see our wrestling heroes perform in the ring. It's dangerous and we should not be hurting each other.

At the same rate, kids have gotten seriously hurt riding bikes, playing on unsafe playgrounds, and eating bad things. It happens. It sucks but kids get do hurt on their journey to adulthood.

Professional wrestling is fun. Why wouldn't we want to try it at home?

In the late 80's, the WWF released "Wrestling Buddies".

These were stuffed doll versions of the times hottest stars.

Even in the commercials we are shown kids trying it at home with these stuffed characters.

There are those on a lower budget who may have attempted moves in classic matches with their pillows.

When you have siblings, performing moves on them is nothing unheard of. Be it big power moves or submissions, there's nothing like striking fear in a loved one with an ill-performed power bomb on a bunk bed.

A kid might find themselves in a professional wrestling inspired war between friends in their neighborhood or school.

Then there are kids who get a little more organized and a lot dumber when creating full-on backyard wrestling companies.

In the late 90's and early 2000's there were an absurd amount of backyard wrestlers performing the hardcore styled wrestling as they saw on television.

This included big leaps, chair shots to the head, and ridiculous uses of weaponry.

Thankfully this fad has faded, but the world of backyard hardcore wrestling still lingers out there in some parts.

No one should be getting hurt when fantasizing about being a professional wrestler like the ones they love on television, but "trying it at home" is always fun.

40. THE SPANISH ANNOUNCE TABLE

Once upon a time, the world only knew what they knew.

We would blend in with our surroundings and our life experiences were very limited.

Thanks to globalization, the day of cultural isolation is over. We have taken advantage of technology and high-speed travel to understand, accept, and experience other lifestyles.

Michael Jackson didn't just create music that his native American audience loved. He created music that everyone across the world would go on to love.

If someone says Michael Jordan in any country, you will find fans of his amazing athleticism.

A great movie is a great movie no matter if one is watching it in a language they know or reading subtitles to comprehend the creative narrative.

The WWE fan base spans all over the globe, and according to them is a universe of its own, but the native tongue of the company is English.

To cater to the universe of fans, the WWE has various commentators calling in the action in different languages.

One of the longest bilingual experiences is that of the Spanish announcers.

They call the action for the Spanish speaking fans at their own table at ringside.

If you've watched wrestling for years or months, you know this because of the tradition of destroying their table on a regular basis.

101 REASONS TO LOVE PRO WRESTLING

The Spanish announce table might as well have a target on it.

In most Pay Per Views and many televised events, the superstars of the company will use it in their match as a weapon.

Going back to Bret Hart being launched through it by Diesel at the 1995 Survivor Series, this four-legged piece of furniture has seen copious amounts of destruction.

Iconic Spanish announcer Carlos Cabrera's knee was clipped in the Bret Hart/Diesel incident and still carries scars from the experience today. He still calls matches and has seen his table destroyed more times than anyone can count.

The fans of WWE have grown to expect it to happen, and the Spanish Announce Table has become as part of the show as almost the ring ropes themselves.

Mick Foley fell off a cell onto it at King of the Ring 98.

Shane McMahon uses it for his huge leaping elbow drop in most of his matches.

John Cena has given many a' Attitude Adjustments through it.

The Shield dealt out plenty group power bombs through it.

Randy Orton is known to use it for his signature RKO finishing move.

Even The Rock has dropped his share of opponents through it with The Rock Bottom.

Fans of professional wrestling that are of legal age can vouch for this.

The ongoing drinking game of taking a shot when the Spanish announcers table breaks has left many feeling 'mucho bueno'.

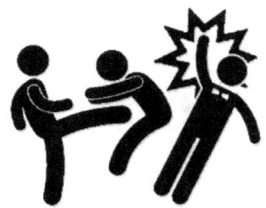

41. THE REF BUMP

All organized competition enforces rules and regulations.

This keeps the contest fair and sets the standard in terms of how to win.

To achieve this objective a judge or official will oversee the contest. Their job is to enforce the rules and maintain the honor of the game.

Baseball has umpires, basketball has refs, and boxing and UFC has both referees and judges.

In most cases these figures become part of the background of the spectacle.

However, that's not always the case.

Sometimes a ref is so intertwined in the game that they fall victim to the physicality of sports.

No one should want to see someone get really hurt, but there is a collective love for seeing a ref get wiped out, a ref taking a baseball to the nether regions, or really any time a ref takes a hit.

In professional wrestling this is the ref bump.

In wrestling it happens fairly often and we fans love every minute of this storytelling contraption.

The wrestling battle gets to the boiling point that it is inevitable that the ending is coming. The energy in the air is electric and every emotion has been expressed.

Then a move gets reversed, someone gets whipped into a corner, or someone lands from a big move and the referee is in the way.

101 REASONS TO LOVE PRO WRESTLING

The referee takes a fall leaving the match without an official.

This allows for the story to go in various iconic directions that longtime fans are well familiar with.

The heel will take advantage of this situation and cheat with a weapon or low blow.

Someone from the outside will interfere to attack a rival in attempt of physical punishment and to control the outcome.

Or the face overcomes the obstacle a foot. They dodge the weapon, take out the outside interference, and have their foe down for a three count.

The crowd erupts with a blaring silence.

The ref is still out. The face is both panicked and a rocket of momentum.

They slap the mat and count to three themselves as the crowd chants along.

The face gives up his pinning position and tends to the fallen ref to help them to their feet. In some cases, another referee will run down to the ring to replace them.

Then out of nowhere the heel rolls up the anxious inertia that is the face.

The ref somehow is now fully alert and counts 1... 2... Whatever may come.

This is a ring ritual that is one of the oldest tropes of the art form used to tell the story.

You can knock down a referee, hit someone with a chair and then cover up your opponent. Then out of nowhere the ref will "wake up" and then count the three. You don't get that anywhere else!

If it's done wrong, then it looks bad.

If it's right, it's one of the best and truest tricks to pull to truly antagonize the emotion of the crowd.

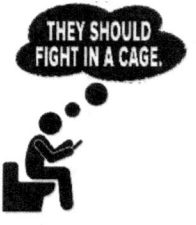

42. FANTASY BOOKING

There has always been a sense of nobility in predicting the future based on both predetermined patterns and absolute creativity.

Nostradamus made very poetic, and what some would consider a little too coincidental, predictions about the future to be coincidental.

The great intellectuals have all had thoughts on where they either thought the world was headed or where they would like it to go.

Weathermen predict when it's going to rain based on patterns and fact.

A psychic will tell you the future based on unknown factors.

When you're a fan of sports, it is likely to fall somewhere in between weatherman and psychic.

The nickname for predicting the future and what one considers the best outcome is the "armchair quarterback".

Fans will boast their so-called expertise and express how things should turn out before it happens.

However, the concept of fantasy booking goes beyond just thinking a dream match would be fun to watch.

Sometimes we enjoy an exhilarating discussion of fantasy booking.

In professional wrestling's glory days, the story lines were never written by Hollywood writers. It was done by a booker or booking committee. The booker decides what happens and the direction of characters, stories, and championship reigns.

101 REASONS TO LOVE PRO WRESTLING

In the entertainment world this is akin fan fiction. It's when super fans take an existing creative property including existing characters and the existing world that has been created to write out their own hypothetical plots.

It's a tribute to the creative world of television, cinema, or in this case professional wrestling.

Fans of wrestling know their ideas will rarely ever be considered.

Those who present professional wrestling shows is doing so because they already have their vision of wrestling, they want to share.

It's kids on a playground, fans at an independent show, fans at a WWE show, older folks, writers, casual fans, other wrestlers, and even celebrities.

Everyone has their own version of what they think wrestling should be.

It's a testament to the passion a fan of the art has and one of the most popular and best forms of discussions a fan can have.

You get to let your mind wander through hypothetical big matches, the "what ifs", and just come up with your own fantasy scenarios.

And super fans get to do this every single week as new programming is pumped out by the biggest promotions.

Any longtime fan of wrestling will be able to tell you their dream matches or what they'd want to do if they could write the story lines themselves.

When the stories in wrestling accomplish their goals, fans get lost in the moment and react accordingly.

Then as soon as the brain processes the reality those aforementioned "what ifs" are always sure to follow.

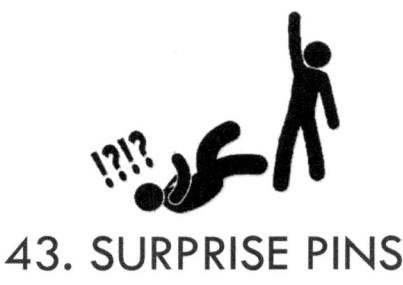

43. SURPRISE PINS

The underdog has always had their moments of overcoming the roadblocks in front of them.

In literature, Robin Hood defeats the Sheriff of Nottingham.

Dark horse underdogs have become president.

Movies about overcoming the odds overcame their own odds and have won Oscars.

They have won professional sport championships and are embedded in our collective rooting spirit.

In professional wrestling the dark horse, the underdogs, and one-time faceless nobodies occasionally jolt the world.

Wrestling has a common trend of finishing matches the same way.

It's almost always a big finishing move and then the winner gets the pin.

Sometimes they'll stall it for dramatic effect, but it's almost always like this.

The "surprise" in surprise pins is a reaction due to the winner being very unexpected.

Be it a "schoolboy" or a "small package", a wrestler will quickly get the pin and stun the opponent, announcer, crowd, and often themselves.

It's common to see the underdog get the quick win but there's other contraptions in this feature of professional wrestling fandom.

It could be a debut of someone that many would not take very seriously.

But there have been tons of examples of big debuts with surprising results.

There has been a plethora of surprise pins in modern wrestling.

Barry Horowitz earned a slap on the back for defeating the overly cocky heel Skip in 1995.

In 1995, long time lovable jobber Mikey Whipwreck actually defeated Steve Austin in ECW before moving on to the WWF and becoming "Stone Cold".

In 2003, The Rock would be upset by The Hurricane.

The established tag team wrestler and future ring general Shelton Benjamin beat a surprised Triple H on a RAW in 2004.

Occasionally, a surprise pin doesn't involve an underdog, but rather just a purely unexpected result.

The biggest shock and awe of a surprise pin occurred at WrestleMania 30 when Brock Lesnar became the "one in 21 and one" while ending Undertaker's WrestleMania winning streak of over twenty years.

No one ever expected Jinder Mahal to defeat Randy Orton, that alone defeat him for the World Title.

But when we're talking about surprise pins there is one that goes down in history as one of the most shocking and most career-making.

In May of 1993, Razor Ramon would take a quick pin from a young skinny guy with a wet mullet.

This was the episode of RAW that established the 1-2-3 Kid as a mainstay in the mainstream.

It can't happen all the time, but when a surprise pin does, it's always a fun shock to the system and everyday happenings.

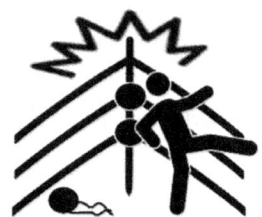

44. THE EXPOSED TURNBUCKLE

A professional wrestling ring is typically constructed the same way every time.

Similar to a boxing ring, the poetically dubbed "squared circle" is 16 to 20 feet squared with four ropes connected to four corner posts.

Each of the twelve rope corners are connected to said corner post with an eyehook named a turnbuckle.

Each of these twelve turnbuckles are wrapped with a turnbuckle pad, a soft covering to protect the wrestlers from colliding with exposed steel.

Sometimes the padding is removed by an opportunist looking to illegally gain the upper hand in a match.

This is the phenomenon of the exposed turnbuckle.

It's addition via subtraction in a bizarre way.

A top turnbuckle pad is "accidentally" removed or straight up ripped off by the bad guy.

When one cannot find a chair or sneak in a foreign object, the exposed turnbuckle is easily accessible by merely untying it from the post.

Then there's an oh-so-suspenseful cat and mouse game where there is that inevitable moment of someone's head connecting with the raw steel of the exposed turnbuckle.

Sometimes the scoundrel who ripped the pad off will succeed in getting their good-guy-enemy's head to collide and then the three-count victory to follow.

There are also those moments where the villain's evil plans backfire.

By being outwitted or a move reversed, it's their cranium that crashes into the exposed ring construct.

Whichever competitor takes the steel hit to the done typically loses.

Lights out!

This has been going on for decades. It's as historic as a rake to eyes or low blow and has been another fun way for wrestlers to tell their in-ring stories.

Andre the Giant would start his match with Jake "The Snake" Roberts' by launching his head into the exposed buckle at WrestleMania V, but its roots go back deep into the territory days of old.

It always seems to pop up at WrestleMania events like WrestleMania XI when Psycho Sid removed it on Shawn Michael's behalf only for the "Heart Break Kid" to still end up losing to the champion Diesel.

This would happen many more times, including WrestleMania 32 when Kalisto retained the United States Championship over Ryback after the pad was ripped off and it went to his advantage.

It just always seems to pop up when watching old matches and still to this day on new programming.

The storytelling contraption of an exposed turnbuckle doesn't occur in every match, or even every show, but when it does it achieves the goal of working up the crowd into a justice-seeking frenzy.

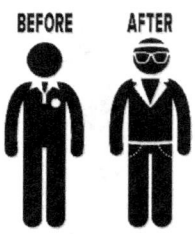

45. REINVENTED CHARACTERS

Cultures change. People change. The world itself as we know it, changes.

When this occurs, one has two choices: adapt or watch it pass you by.

Actors will change up their look and character performance for each role they land.

An athlete might switch jersey numbers or add some questionable tattoos to change-up their appearance.

The persona that connects to their art can get a little more creative to meet the visual demands of their audience.

Musicians do this all the time.

Rockstar icons like David Bowie went from human to alien to whatever he wanted, The Beatles went from clean-cut mop-tops to hippies, and even Elvis went from standard 50's garb to sequined capes and jumpers.

Of course, there's the likes of a Madonna or Lady Gaga switching it up and keeping their pop-star images interesting and a talking point.

Sean Combs has gone from Puff Daddy to P-Diddy, and all of the sameness in between. But at least his branding was changed.

Change is never a bad thing.

It allows a reset, an opportunity to stay interesting, new visuals to sell new merchandise, and a chance to engage a crowd in a new way.

In professional wrestling, this can easily happen with a reinvented character.

101 REASONS TO LOVE PRO WRESTLING

A reinvented character can be renaissance of one a performer's career or just another destination on the journey on their career.

Sometimes an act will get stale or just never connect with the crowd. What will sometimes happen is that these people will get a second chance.

The performer gets to re-debut as a new repackaged character or come back with a refreshed version of what they've already established.

The character-driven performance that is professional wrestling thrives on renovation, evolution, and capturing the imaginations of its viewers.

A reinvented character is a proven way to do this.

Sometimes it's just evolving from the lower card to the Main Event.

Steve Austin was "Stunning" and "The Ringmaster" before becoming "Stone Cold".

Triple H went from a Connecticut Snob to "Cerebral Assassin" on his way to being a multi-time World Champion.

Glenn Jacobs would portray various characters before the WWF, but he'd also play various characters IN the WWF. He started as an evil dentist named Isaac Yankem before moving on to a fake version of Diesel and then finally former World Champion and Undertaker's brother Kane.

Now he's a Mayor in Tennessee.

Certain characters do work, but also don't meet the expectations or needs of a wrestling company's story. Freshening up is vital in these cases.

Hulk Hogan rode out his All-American red and yellow character for years on the highest level a wrestler could. To rejuvenate his character, he turned on the fans and embraced a new "Hollywood" Hogan persona.

Bray Wyatt came in as a southern cult leader and renovated his character into the bizarre fun that is the Firefly Fun House and the horror monster The Fiend. His character continues to ever evolve.

Sting started off as a colorful face-painting surfer for the early part of his career before striking gold by copying the movie "The Crow" and then striking cold with ripping off "The Joker" in TNA.

Mick Foley was Cactus Jack, Mankind, Dude Love, and eventually just himself.

Then there's those who never quite make it to the top of the card but celebrate longevity because of their ability to get different characters over with the crowd.

Charles Wright started off as Papa Shango in the early 90's and would go on to be "The Supreme Fighting Machine" Kama before developing his most popular character "The Godfather".

Scott Hall was one of the best of all time and is a Hall of Famer, but he grew from The Diamond Stud in AWA, to Razor Ramon in WWF, and then the nWo version of Scott Hall in WCW.

Chris Jericho has pretty much always been Chris Jericho, but he has changed his character up every couple of years to remain fresh and extend his already legendary career.

The same can be said for Matt Hardy, Dustin Rhodes, Raven, Barry Darsow, and many others who have continued to hone their craft inside the ring while renovating their personas.

Just about everyone in professional wrestling that has had a long career has changed their on-screen character up a bit to stay relevant.

The facade of a wrestler is essential to business.

A character must resonate with the audience or serve a purpose within the on-going story.

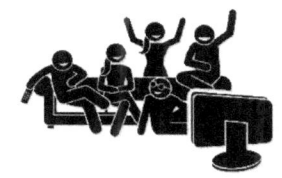

46. SUPER CARDS

Big events are nothing new in the world of sports.

The NFL has the Superbowl. The NBA has the Finals, Baseball has the World Series, soccer has the World Cup, and the entire world has the Olympics.

Professional wrestling has super cards.

These are the highly promoted and highly anticipated shows that feature the big rivals come head to head, historic championship matches, and the largest crowd of rapid fans that have been waiting for these shows to come.

Super cards go back to the early days of professional wrestling.

There was always the big payoff for big matches that would often lead to big events at big venues and sometimes even baseball stadiums.

When wrestling began to become a televised production, it was safe to predict that televised super cards were on their way.

In 1983, Jim Crockett's NWA would unleash Starrcade until the world.

This super card featured the gigantic matchup between "The Nature Boy" Ric Flair and the legendary Harley Race inside of a steel cage. Thousands of fans would fill the Greensboro, North Carolina arena and thousands more would watch at home.

This tradition would continue for decades as Starrcade would be the biggest show for Crockett's promotion and then WCW.

More super cards would be added to the calendar that fans could and would look forward to for months.

101 REASONS TO LOVE PRO WRESTLING

Then Pay Per View became a thing. The people at home could pay a fee and tune in from the comfort of their own couch from anywhere in the world.

With this, the concept of WrestleMania took the crown of the king of super cards. Since the early 1980's, the WWF and then WWE have held their annual super card.

WrestleMania has become the Superbowl of professional wrestling. And rightfully so. This spectacle has featured the biggest of stars in the biggest of matches in front of the biggest of crowds. Even if someone doesn't know much about wrestling, they know that WrestleMania is a "big deal".

It's just one of those universal events. The fact that the carny business of wrestling has evolved and built up an event SO MUCH that they can draw over 80,000 people, sell millions on PPV, and virtually control an entire major city for one weekend a year, says a lot.

That's not even looking at the impact of the actual narrative side of the business. When you get into that area your mind will wander in awe for hours.

The grandiose awe of super cards is not reserved to the history of WWE and WCW.

Extreme Championship Wrestling, Ring of Honor, Impact Wrestling, and now All Elite Wrestling have all presented their own super cards.

And it doesn't end with American based wrestling promotions. Mexico, Japan, and elsewhere have all had their own super card events.

Fans of professional wrestling are fortunate to be able to form their own memories with any given show, but it is the super cards that the collective memories and moments that bring us together... and make our favorite promotions a lot of money.

It's something to look forward to. It's a platform for legends to be made. It's both the end of a chapter and the start of a new. It's a super card and it's the event you never want to miss.

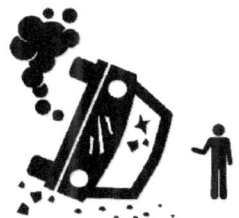

47. AUTO DESTRUCTION

The Ford Model T, the first mass produced automobile, was launched in 1908.

This innovation would have a large impact on society as we know it.

With personal cars came trucks and other modes of transportation.

With the growth of automobiles, auto racing became a global pastime.

Spectators would watch to see who would win the race, but at the same the shock and awe of a big crash is what many would be talking about the following day.

This strange fascination would evolve into monster truck rallies where gigantic trucks would ram into each other, run over junk cars, and totally embrace the automotive carnage that fans would cheer for.

Then there are demolition derbies. Where old cars are, well... demolished.

If fans of anything are cheering, of course professional wrestling listens.

And since, wrestling has seen its share of automotive destruction.

Brawling in a parking lot is a thing of old. When you're fighting around thousands of pounds of potential carnage, that potential was often reached.

During the Attitude Era, the WWE would see more auto destruction than the worst of winter pileups.

Whether it was "Stone Cold" Steve Austin filling Vince McMahon's fancy Corvette with cement in 1998, "Stone Cold" Steve Austin running The Rock's new car with a monster truck in 99, or even "Stone Cold" Steve Austin blowing up the DX Express by dropping a steel beam on it in

2000... auto destruction was here to stay and that was the bottom line because SOMEONE said so.

WCW was no stranger to the auto destruction phenomenon at this time as they had the "White Hummer" mystery, where said hummer destroyed a limo where Kevin Nash was hanging out.

In 2001, Triple H totaled Undertaker's motorcycle with his trusty sledgehammer.

In 2005, Batista would smash up JBL's limo.

Then three years later, John Cena and Cryme Tyme would also vandalize JBL's white limo.

In 2007, Vince McMahon's limo would explode. Luckily, he didn't die... or walk away with a scratch at all. We'll ignore that one.

In 2009, Kofi Kingston would destroy Randy Orton's new race car with a tire iron and bucket of paint.

In 2017, Brawn Strowman would LIFT and destroy an ambulance.

It goes on and on and will continue to do so.

It's just one of those things.

For some reason it's become perfectly acceptable for any and all on-camera cars, trucks, limos, and modes of transportation to be vandalized... to the roaring joy of the fans.

48. CREATURE FEATURES

Everyone should have a spirit animal.

This is an animal that one relates to and can focus on to gain energy, inspiration, or comfort.

"Fight Club" saw Marla delve into the world of penguins.

"Donny Darko" was spoken to by Frank the Bunny.

The Flintstones had a dinosaur. The Jetsons, a dog. And Sabrina the Teenage Witch had a talking black cat.

It would be hard not to feel empowered by the majesty of a soaring eagle. It would be unheard of to not love a cute and cuddly panda. It would be nonsense to hate on someone for loving their dog.

Animals are part of nature and so are we.

There is a plethora of domesticated animals that we welcome into our homes and welcome into our hearts.

A professional wrestler might be larger than life, big and bad, and with a presence to them that leaves those they encounter in speechless awe.

They are still human and part of the greater nature that is our ecological society.

This means professional wrestlers will not shy themselves from presenting their own creature features.

Jake Roberts was a wrestler from Georgia, but Jake "The Snake" Roberts is a legend. With his snake Damien, Jake ate up the scenery in the 1980's.

The tag team British Bulldogs not only used Bulldogs as their gimmick but brought out their own little cute bulldog in "Matilda".

A man named Koko B. Ware sounds like a fun person just based off the name. But when you add a parrot named Frankie, the act goes from forgettable to Hall of Fame worthy.

Ricky Steamboat is one of the most impressive and respected pro wrestlers of all time, but Ricky "The Dragon" Steamboat made it a lot easier to sell some shirts.

Animals are part of wrestling character gimmicks going even beyond those who include the literal animal into their act.

There was The Junkyard Dog, George "The Animal" Steel, The Killer Bees, and Hawk and Animal from Legion of Doom from the 80's.

"Stone Cold" Steve Austin was nicknamed the "Rattlesnake". Randy Orton is the "Viper". There's a Rhyno and even a Shark Boy.

Professional wrestling is a lot like going to a zoo.

You will see animals and creature features.

And just like the zoo, you never want to see anyone escape from their cage.

101 REASONS TO LOVE PRO WRESTLING

49. MANAGERS

Fighters have had managers going back to the early days of organized combat.

These businesspeople would organize, promote, and take care of their fighter going into the big match-up.

Boxing managers are mentors, advisers, and guides that look out for the best interest of their fighter.

And, of course, since it is a business, they'd get their cut of the fighter's income.

Jackie Kallen would be one of the first and most successful female managers once she entered the business ranks in the 1970's.

We've seen this in movies as well. There is almost always a force behind the force.

In professional wrestling, the role of the manager is similar... but a little different.

A manager will walk to the ring with their wrestler and, depending on if they are good or evil, get involved.

There have been iconic exceptions to the rule, but the role of a professional wrestling manager is often reserved for bad guys.

This allows a heel that may not be as skilled on the microphone to have a mouthpiece that can help hype their status or matches.

Then there are bodyguards who act as the heel wrestler's enforcer to give them a physical upper hand.

101 REASONS TO LOVE PRO WRESTLING

Shawn Michaels had Diesel, The Four Horsemen had their own enforcer in the form of Arn Anderson, and Chris Jericho had Ralphus.

Some of the greats have had a female valet at ringside to act as a distraction or get their own hands dirty to ensure the unhanded victory.

The Hall of Famers "Sensational" Sherri, "Sunny" Tammy Sytch, Chyna, and a slew of others have carved their path taking this route.

A manager can work with tag teams and believe me they have.

The most successful tag team manager of all time is undeniable.

Jim Cornette, as polarizing as he is, is by far the most successful heel tag team manager.

But he's not alone.

Paul Ellering was the vocal backbone of the Road Warriors.

Certain managers are a little more ambitious and take on a whole stable of wrestlers to assist and guide.

Some of the best ever in "The Mouth from the South" Jimmy Hart, Bobby "The Brain" Heenan, and Paul Heyman have shared their services amongst a group of heels.

They might be former wrestlers, huge fans, or just very skilled performers but the persona of a professional wrestling manager definitely has its place.

They are easy to hate, easy to boo, and easy to get the invested.

When they finally get their comeuppance, whether it be seeing their fighter lose, finally take their deserved lickings, or are just embarrassed, the crowd always goes home happy.

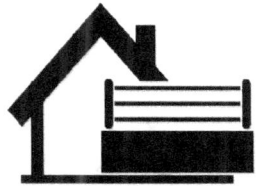

50. HOUSE SHOWS

Long before televised productions, pay per views, premium live events, and live streaming options, professional wrestling was a touring act.

A stand-up comedian goes town to town telling the same jokes and a band touring goes stage to stage playing the same set list every night.

The same script will be used every night when a play is being performed.

Professional wrestling has more similarities to these traditions than many would think.

Tracing back to its traveling carnival roots and a traveling vaudeville act, professional wrestling would always make it's rounds.

With these unconnected shows it was easy to put together an entertaining card. A wrestling promotion would showcase the same wrestlers in the same matches, with often the same results. Then on to the next town 100 miles away with the same exact presentation.

This was before the days of everyone being privy of every result that happens on any given night. These fans didn't know or care because the show, right there in front of them, was exciting and something to look forward to.

This would result in wrestling feuds lasting for months and years and since the performers were facing off every night, they could put together a match that would entertain the audience more than a normal one-off.

These shows were also a chance to have big title matches, as advertised on the early studio wrestling shows.

But times change. Televised productions, pay per views, and live streaming options on top of the internet providing more coverage than ever before these shows would see a change.

However, these house shows wouldn't be too far off. It would be common to see the same big main events night after night, the same mid card matches, and same copy-and-paste production.

But there is still magic to a modern-day house show. You get to see the performers you watch on TV before your very eyes. The good guys win, the bad guys lose, and the fans go home happy and yearning for their next live event experience.

Then sometimes the promotions throw a huge curve ball at us. A championship match will not go as expected and a new champion will be crowned.

This is not something that is taken for granted. Sometimes contracts end, someone gets in real-life trouble, or there is an internal decision that a change is needed, and it's needed despite the event not being televised.

Bret "The Hitman" Hart's first WWF World title reign came after defeating "Nature Boy" Ric Flair at a house show in 1992.

Diesel would defeat Bob Backlund for the WWF World Title in 94.
Tag team titles would swap around.

Women's Championships have switched. Mid card titles like the WWE Intercontinental and WCW's Television title would move on to new owners and back and forth.

Even the NXT World Title would change owners twice at house shows. It's these moments that turn a house show into an event for the history books. It's these moments that keep the "anything can happen" vibe alive.

Of course, 9 times out of 10, you're getting the same show from the town before... but that's the magic of a professional wrestling house show.

On any given night, an upset or surprise can happen. And that's what keeps us going back for more.

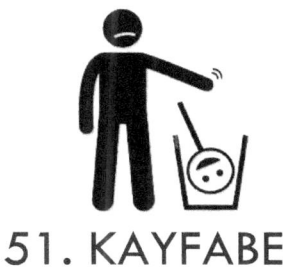

51. KAYFABE

There are cultural norms that we just have to accept.

One of these norms is pretending for the sake of the children.

We pretend that their little faces are going to get stuck like that because seeing them make goofy faces can become tedious.

We pretend to children that school does indeed not suck because we know the value of education.

We pretend that certain holiday figures are real to children to give them something joyous to look forward.

But what if that magic of being 'pretended to' didn't have do end?

It doesn't. At any age we can suspend belief.

It's a monster in a haunted house. It's getting lost in a great TV show or extra engaging video game. It's letting oneself enter a different reality to experience some magic.

But there is someone behind the monster mask. There is someone writing that great TV show and someone programming that extra engaging video game.

And to experience magic, a magician has their code. A code to protect the workings of making the illusion work.

Professional wrestling has its own magician code in the form of a culture that is called Kayfabe.

Kayfabe is the inside norms that the fraternity and sorority of professional wrestlers partake in to provide the magic and illusion that IS professional wrestling.

Basically, Kayfabe is maintaining the reality that what a fan sees in real.

Professional wrestlers will use a glossary of terms to describe things that occur in their world.

They will even use a cross between pig-Latin and Snoop Dogg's "izzle" talk that is aptly called "speaking Carny".

There's even a handshake.

In older days, Kayfabe would be taken seriously with it being against the rules to allow a good guy and bad guy to be seen together in public.

Injuries would be presented as real on the streets.

Good guys would be good, while bad guys would be bad.

These rockstars would tour the world presenting themselves as the characters the fans paid to see.

There is the modern argument that Kayfabe is dead.

The modern fan goes behind the curtain of Kayfabe and uses those insider terms, dive deep into ratings of the television shows, listen to industry-made podcasts, watch movies and shows that delve into the behind the scenes stories, and well, most fans think they know everything.

But do they really?

It's easy to say 'Yes, the business has been exposed.'

Kayfabe as it was once known may have been buried alive, but this does not mean the illusion is resting in peace.

Professional wrestlers will still blur the lines of reality by utilizing social media to rile up the fans, injury comebacks still surprise us, the anticipation for results are still intact, and there is always going to be things fans will not really know about that happens behind the curtain.

While world adapts and things change, kayfabe has merely evolved.

Professional wrestlers were once rockstar superheroes that abided by their own magician code. Now? Not so much.

Regardless, abracadabra...

We are all still in on the joke.

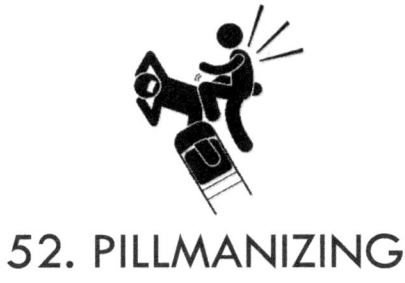

52. PILLMANIZING

Eternalizing someone is nothing new.

Religious deities, war heroes, and iconic figures are immortalized through statues, fine art, and dedicated memorials.

This is also common in sports.

There are professional sport trophies named over past heroes.

And name recognition like saying "Kobe" when sinking a jump shot.

Professional wrestling is no different.

The backstage area behind the entrance curtain is the "Gorilla Position", named after the late great Gorilla Monsoon.

NXT regularly presents the Dusty Rhodes Classic as memorial tournaments have become a celebrated way to carry on the legacy of a fallen icon and friend.

Naming things after those who made an impact in professional wrestling is a way to show respect and let legends live forever.

Another contraption of this is naming certain moves after legends.

There's the Lou Thiez Press. The Gory Guerrero Special. The Vader Bomb and it goes on and on because professional wrestling cherishes tradition.

There is one move, or in this case an act of violence, that is an extreme sight to say the least.

Pillmanizing.

Named after the great Brian Pillman.

Brian Pillman was a professional football player turned WCW "High Flyin'" lightweight trailblazer... turned "Hollywood Blonde" tag team specialist... turned "Loose Cannon" and member of the Four Horsemen.

He would eventually make his way to the WWF, but tragically his life and career would be cut short before he could reach the magnitude that longtime fans knew he could have, and would have, achieved.

He is remembered for his greatness and that includes great matches, great promos, and great moments.

Pillman's name is also etched in the history books for a vicious form of attacking one's enemy.

The concept of Pillmanizing is simple.

Take a limb like an arm or leg... or even one's neck and wrap a folding chair around it.

Then with a leap, sometimes from the ring ropes, the menacing heel stomps the chair.

It fractures arms. It breaks legs. It snaps necks.

It's a visual that leaves a huge impression on the viewer, so it is not a form of attack that is overplayed.

It is typically reserved for heated rivalries and the most personal of personal story lines.

What many fans do not consider is that this attack was not by the hands of Brian Pillman.

One of the most famous professional wrestlers of all time, "Stone Cold" Steve Austin attacked the former "Hollywood Blonde" partner and then bad guy Hart Foundation member in October of 1996.

Austin put Brian Pillman's ankle in a chair and viciously stomped on it.

This would lead to Pillman having an injured ankle for a while to help set up the infamous "Canadian Stampede" tag match that saw Austin and a team of others take on the Hart Foundation.

That's the beauty of professional wrestling.

Heroes and stand outs aren't always the ones who hit the home run or win the championship.

Some icons get an attack named after them...

Even if they were on the receiving end of it.

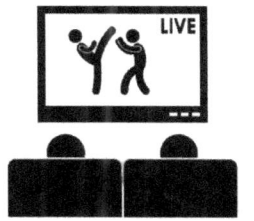

53. CONSISTENT PROGRAMING

We are creatures of habit.

We are children who wake up. Go to school. Come home. Go to sleep.

This becomes waking up. Going to work. Coming to home. Going to sleep.

We fall into this routine until we are old and stop going anywhere at all.

The comforts in between are what keep us going.

Some people take interest in following their favorite sports team. Some get engaged in their favorite television shows. Some nosedive deep into hobbies.

Professional wrestling is all three of those wrapped in one.

We cheer on our favorites just like a sports team. We get engaged in the action. We nosedive deep into the spectacle.

This is all thanks to consistent programming.

Since the dawn of television, professional wrestling has found its way to the airwaves.

Whether it was weekend matinees or closed-circuit big events, wrestling has always been a popular viewing option.

Then Monday nights happened.

On Monday nights, you have RAW.

On Friday nights, you have Smackdown.

101 REASONS TO LOVE PRO WRESTLING

Wednesday is AEW.

There are other shows like NXT, Impact, NWA, or MLW.

Over the past few decades, there have been a wide variety of wrestling shows to tune into.

It does not matter how your week was.

You could have the best week of your life or the worst.

Professional wrestling is there.

It's on television just as it always is and always was.

Wrestling fans are creatures of habit just like everyone else so of course we tune in and tune out.

We get lost in the world of wrestling via the regularly scheduled programing that we love.

There is the rare preemption, but 95% of the time you're going to get your preferred dose of wrestling on a weekly basis.

Sports have an off season and television shows will take vacations or stick to specific seasons.

Not professional wrestling.

It's on all year long.

It's the unhealthiest of comfort foods and it's ALWAYS there when you need it.

54. CREATING NEW FANS

The objective of any business and commercial art form is to expand its exposure.

This is establishing a consumer base for a business and creating more memories and engagement for art.

Any entity that has a continuously forming history and cemented ritual needs one thing to survive.

Followers.

It does not just happen.

We do not just wake up into consciousness with a passion for sports or knowledge of religion.

There must be a catalyst to ignite this in us.

We are influenced by others, and geography, on what sport team we want to win, or how one decides to pray, if at all.

Like zombies, we go for the brains around us: not to eat but to influence.

There are many reasons we humans chant "One of us. One of us." and of course professional wrestling is one of them.

Wrestling fandom has many routes to enter from.

There are the odd, but not unheard of, cases where someone will just casually come across it on their own and become enthralled in the action.

But more fans than not are created by exposure from a third party.

101 REASONS TO LOVE PRO WRESTLING

A friend could show you matches that pique your interest.

A grandmother or anyone from your family could have it on and a superhero-like character could grab your eyes.

It is how those halls, arenas, and stadiums fill their seats.

It is how advertisers, television stations, and sponsors measure the value of business professional wrestling provides.

It is how the tradition carries on.

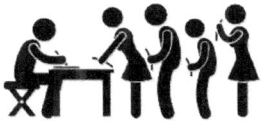

55. CONVENTIONS

When we enjoy things, we like enjoying it with like-minded people.

Political conventions have been around in America since before the Declaration of Independence was signed.

Fans of specific genres of entertainment and art have gathered to share in their passions.

Going back to the 1930's when the "Philcon", or the Philadelphia Science Fiction Conference, was established for sci-fi fans to gather, mingle with its creative leaders, and to celebrate their collective interest.

Fan conventions would continue to cover science fiction but other industries and hobbies as well.

These events would evolve with the times, to the point that the San Diego Comic Con would become a pivotal piece of entertainment and fandom.

If there has ever been a way to capitalize off fandom, professional wrestling is right there.

Going back to the mid-1960's, professional wrestling has showcased its own fan conventions.

While the Cauliflower Alley Club was either the first or one of the firsts, the idea of wrestling fan conventions has taken a life of its own.

A professional wrestling convention gives fans a chance to get autographs and photos with past and present heroes, often for a fee, participate in interviews, take in memorabilia displays, and often take in some matches.

The biggest are often attached to a big event.

The WWE capitalizes on fans from across the globe coming in for big events like WrestleMania or Summer Slam with their Axxess events.

Other smaller companies will piggy-back off these shows and have their own events and fan conventions in the same towns at the same time.

There is also WrestleCon, Starrcast, WrestleCade, and many more that have or continue to hold big conventions with both regional and international appeal.

When a die-hard fan eats, sleeps, and breathes professional wrestling it is not even a question about attending.

They will attend.

They will stand in long lines and often pay for a brief moment with their heroes.

Outside of the shows themselves there are not that many events that embrace a community of fans with memory-making experiences.

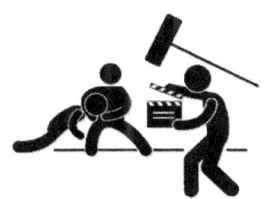

56. HOLLYWOOD INTERPRETATIONS

As soon as the motion pictures of Hollywood began, there have been real life interruptions.

There have been movies about presidents, sports heroes, artists, and historic moments.

If it's interesting and provides cinematic value, there are a few thousand miles of film dedicated to it.

The production that is professional wrestling is something that is already cinematic so it would only make sense for the world of cinema to want to present their own rendition of it.

Professional wrestling has had a plethora of Hollywood interpretations since the dawn of the motion picture.

There are many times where a wrestling event is part of the background of a movie or television show.

Movies like the underrated Michael J. Fox classic "Life with Mikey" featured a scene where the film's characters were at an event featuring Jerry "the King" Lawler.

"The Fonz" himself, Henry Winkler was a professional wrestler in the 1978 film "The One and Only"

Sitcoms like "Boy Meets World", "Mama's Family", and "Family Matters" all saw the characters on their shows tangle with professional wrestlers in the ring.

Triple H would appear on both "The Drew Carey Show" AND "The Bernie Mac Show".

101 REASONS TO LOVE PRO WRESTLING

"Stone Cold" Steve Austin would appear in the form of claymation for "Celebrity Death Match".

Even The Rock has a sitcom centering around his life and played his own father on an episode of "That 70's Show".

Then there are cinematic depictions that center around the world that is wrestling.

In 2006, Jack Black starred as the title character "Nacho Libre", a silly comedy that is about a lucha libre character.

Mickey Rourke starred in the 2008 film "The Wrestler" that showed a more realistic look at the life of a wrestler clinging on to mild success.

The Netflix show "GLOW" touched on the history of the Gorgeous Ladies of Wrestling to both critical and fan acclaim.

The WWE also had their own film division that has delved into the world of wrestling and even outside of it. But no matter what, their productions feature famous wrestlers getting their acting on.

The magic of a rolling camera is that virtually anything could be the topic that is being presented.

There is no reason professional wrestling can't have some of that spotlight.

As long as the production respects the art of what wrestling is, professional wrestling fans will tune in and watch.

101 REASONS TO LOVE PRO WRESTLING

57. SNEAK ATTACKS

Any entity at war seeks an advantage over their opponent.

Catching them off guard is a great way gain that said advantage.

The sneak attack is used to gain the upper hand over someone by attacking them when they least expect it.

Sometimes it's just a reckless attack of a fed-up foe.

Other times, most of time, it's when a bad guy knows they can't defeat their enemy on a normal face to face manner.

They resort to the cheap antic of sneaking in their attack.

It's not always a situation of bad guys being bad.

A sneak attack could actually have various reactions.

Like the Trojan Horse at your door, when a sneak attack by is considered "good", the good guys are cheered on.

But most sneak attacks are considered as something negative like Pearl Harbor.

The difference is there, but the sneak attack in wrestling has had more of a connection with bad guys than good guys.

It's considered underhanded, cheap, and disgraceful when someone attacks someone from behind.

It's something the malicious Four Horsemen would do to gain the upper hand against their rivals.

At the same rate, if it's the rare case when a good guy utilizes this practice.

Then it's seen as a big moment of comeuppance like when "Stone Cold" Steve Austin would pop up and sneak attack bad guy rivals like The Rock or Mr. McMahon.

There is also the horrific moment when a good guy uses a sneak attack to turn on their fellow good guy.

It can be as simple as an evil cowboy not following the rules of a showdown.

Or it could be a vicious ambush.

This is part of the life a professional wrestling character lives out.

This could also be why professional wrestling characters are so bizarre.

Because when they least expect it, the next sneak attack could come out of nowhere.

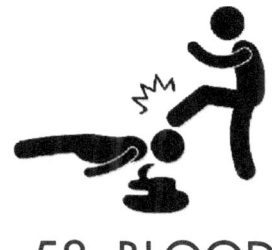

58. BLOOD

As a primal element of our existence, blood is something humanity holds in a pretty high regard.

Humans and a lot of other living beings' function thanks to the blood that flows inside them.

This red liquid life force brings oxygen to the body as is the fuel that the heart beats on.

It's a necessity for life and the lineage we carry in it is our ancestral history.

In the arts, blood is what a vampire drinks from their prey.

In fact, there are few horror genre movies that doesn't feature bloodstained scenes.

In acts of violence, blood is drawn.

This graphic scene is always alarming, but hard to forget.

This visual also has an infamous history in professional wrestling.

The visual awe that is blood in wrestling lets the audience know that the match their watching is a serious fight.

In older days, wrestlers would get busted open "the hard way".

This means they would connect a few well-placed punches above the eyebrow to give the presentation that bloody visual.

This can result in a trickle, or it could provide a full on crimson mask.

Other generations of wrestlers would use a concealed piece of razor blade to slice themselves.

Blading, Gigging, Juicing, or whatever term is preferred has caused its share of shock and awe, in efforts to tell the most compelling story and to sell a match that much more.

There are even times a cut goes too deep, and a bloody face becomes a full-on bloodbath.

Which of these methods is more barbaric is up for debate, but the endgame is still the same.

The dramatic effect of seeing blood in a match gives it the suspension of disbelief an extra layer of realism.

We know the value of blood, so when it's spilled it's often spilled for a reason.

Like anything, there is excess in wrestling.

Some shows will have blood every other match and it will be an overdone gore fest.

But in most cases, this is reserved for heated rivalries and big moments.

Some wrestlers had more of these big moments and had the scar tissue to prove it.

Most fans of professional wrestling are not blood lusting animals.

But it's in anyone's nature to understand the severity of blood.

There are specific visuals that longtime fans will never forget.

"Stone Cold" Steve Austin at WrestleMania 13.

"Cactus Jack" Mick Foley in those Japanese Death Matches.

Terry Funk being Terry Funk.

Ric Flair's blonde locks always being soaked.

Brock Lesnar beating the blood out of John Cena and Randy Orton.

The Great Muta going way too far with it in 1992.

There has been many many more gallons poured outside of these examples.

Thankfully, the times have changed.

Blood still happens, but not nearly as much.

We will instantly see a referee put on medical gloves and approach the situation accordingly.

But again, it still happens.

These moments still leave scar tissue on our collective memories.

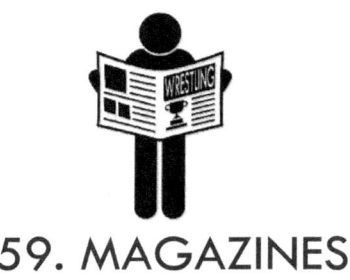

59. MAGAZINES

The written word is a form of communication that has influenced society since symbols left in caves.

There are books, pamphlets, and newspapers.

The written word is used to inspire, entertain, and inform.

The earliest example of a magazine was a philosophy and literary collection launched in Germany during the 1660's.

From there magazines of every possible topic, theme, and lifestyle has made its way from print to shelf.

Then over the past few generations, technology has evolved while the printed word has seen a steep decline.

Professional wrestling has ridden this same wave.

Before the internet, there was not many ways to find out about the world of wrestling outside of shows and often outside of your television signal.

Even before the idea of trading VHS copies of shows with other fans.

There was one way to keep up as much as possible about the world of professional wrestling.

Magazines.

Getting to read about the territories outside of your own was done via reading about it in magazines.

One of the earliest magazines dedicated to professional wrestling was a Chicago, IL magazine titled "Wrestling As You Like It".

It ran from the mid-40's through the mid-50's before becoming "Wrestling Life" and running through the mid-1960's.

"Wrestling Revue" ran from 1959 until 1983.

"Inside Wrestling" and "The Wrestler" ran from 1960s through 2013, surviving a very long time compared to its alternatives.

This also brought us Bill Apter. A photographer turned editor that is credited for carrying the load of professional wrestling publications.

Then one of the most renowned would be "Pro Wrestling Illustrated".

Launched in 1979, the magazine would feature highly acclaimed annual awards, a top 500 wrestlers list, and more that have kept fans talking and definitely kept them buying.

The WWF, WCW, and even ECW would have their own magazines centering around their specific company.

Time would eliminate these publications, as well as most of the companies.

Fans of professional wrestling no longer have to wait for a monthly magazine to arrive in the mail or show up at a newsstand.

The internet came and wiped all of that away.

Information was put at our fingertips on a keyboard and then put in our pockets on a smart phone.

There are still a few out there, but the magazine has seen its best days in the past.

It's still a relic of professional wrestling history that the timeline of super fandom required to get where we are today.

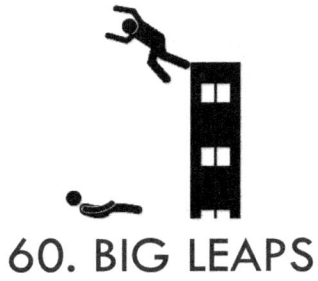

60. BIG LEAPS

There is a sense of adrenaline, fear, and spectacle that goes hand in hand with extreme heights.

There are those who climb mountains, perform as part of trapeze acts, and have occupations that require being high in the air.

Like an astronaut utilizing a spaceship to exit the atmosphere, the human race takes on all limits.

Neil Armstrong's "one small step man, one giant leap for mankind" is embedded in history.

The 'small step part' is cool and all, but it is that 'giant leap' that hits the soul.

In professional wrestling it's not one giant leap for mankind.

It is a giant leap FROM Mankind.

Defying gravity is one of the many feats in professional wrestling that puts fans on the edge of their seats.

Whether it's from the top of a cage or ladder, from the top of a big set piece, or even from an arena balcony or scaffold, professional wrestlers will take a giant leap in order to use their own bodies as a weapon.

Then there's a flip side to this.

Sometimes someone gets thrown from a cage or ladder, from the top of a set piece, or really any other elevated locations.

Throwing yourself off or being thrown off essentially has the same effect.

101 REASONS TO LOVE PRO WRESTLING

There is that collective hush over the crowd.

No one blinks and every breath is held.

Then there's the impact.

The human spaceship lands.

101 REASONS TO LOVE PRO WRESTLING

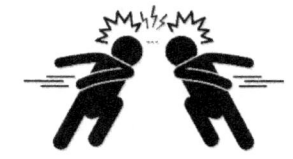

61. BITTER RIVALS

It is a natural instinct to be competitive and with that comes rivalries.

It happens to countries who do not get along.

The bible featured Cain and Abel, two brothers who became rivals.

There are battling brands like Coca Cola and Pepsi or McDonalds and Burger King.

In sports, many teams have bitter rivals.

It is that competitive rivalry that just has the little bit more of hatred and passion.

In the ever-so passionate world of professional wrestling there have been many bitter rivals.

The first bitter rivals like George Hackenschmidt and Frank Gotch were mainly rivals because they were both big box office draws that held on to the top championships.

Then as theatrics came into play, the storyline contraption of a feud could become a bitter rivalry based on how well it was remembered and how well the performers pulled it off.

Terry Funk and Dusty Rhodes made the world cringe at the carnage each man would inflict on the other.

Storied rivalries like Hulk Hogan and Andre the Giant, Ric Flair and Ricky Steamboat, "Stone Cold" Steve Austin and Vince McMahon, Bret Hart and Shawn Michaels, and more have had rivalries that it would hard to not consider bitter.

These are the big matches that people fill arenas, order Pay Per Views for, and creates the folklore that is professional wrestling.

That's just the stuff in front of the camera. Like any industry there is going to be conflict behind the scenes.

This has provided wrestling fans with a whole other level of bitter rivals.

Shawn Michaels and Bret Hart. Bret Hart and Vince McMahon. Vince McMahon and Ted Turner. Vince Russo and Jim Cornette. Hulk Hogan and self-respect.

The rivalries don't end with the scripted show. There are people who just don't like each other, screwed each other over, or were in direct competition.

In a perfect world everyone gets along behind the scenes, but they just don't. And fans just love hearing the dirt.

Then there are times the behind-the-scenes rivalries is turned into a story line, and all is okay. Fun times.

There are points in a wrestler's career when a feud gets so heated that fans just automatically assume they'll still hate each other years down the line.

If you see Hogan and Flair in the ring, you always expect one to attack the other.

If Vince McMahon and Steve Austin are ever in the ring together, under ANY circumstance, it would be expected to see Austin drop a Stunner on him.

Sure, there is a level of mutual respect, but as a fan it's not hard to anticipate the worst.

That's the legend of hate, that will always fill arenas.

101 REASONS TO LOVE PRO WRESTLING

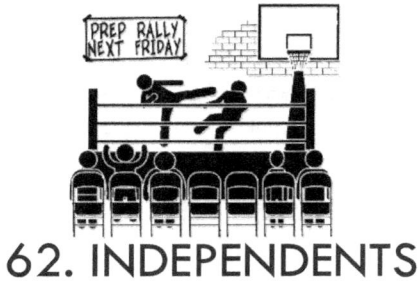

62. INDEPENDENTS

The idea of overnight success is a myth.

Jeff Bezos has said that "real overnight success" actually takes 10 years.

The fresh new actor did a dozen small movies before being a leading man.

A band that's winning Grammys played shows and learned what worked for them and what didn't.

The most hilarious comedian has surely bombed at a local open mic on their way to becoming a household name.

That superstar athlete didn't just show up and win MVP. They formed their skills in school and the early seasons of their careers.

Professional wrestling stars don't automatically show up and get put on television.

Professional wrestling has functioned on a system that is similar to Major League Baseball system.

There are different levels and milestones to level-up.

To make it to the big time or even to grab a one-off background role, almost all roles are casted through the independent wrestling companies.

The biggest companies have the pick of the litter of smaller companies, that are ran independent from the mainstream promotions.

These promotions are often the training grounds for wrestling. The creme rises to the top, becomes champion, and creates a name for them in the towns they perform in.

101 REASONS TO LOVE PRO WRESTLING

The small independent wrestling promotions are made up of people who are chasing their dreams to one day main event WrestleMania and those who are just seeking the life story of being able to say they were once a professional wrestler.

For these wrestlers, it's living out their childhood goals while still maintaining a 9 to 5 job.

These smaller shows are often in bars, community centers, and pretty much anywhere a ring can be set up and the locals can gather.

The best of this level travel from area to area, working for different independent wrestling promotions with the goal of getting noticed by a large company that can offer them a full-time contract.

Then like the minor league baseball system, there are those who are in their way down.

These wrestlers have made it to the mainstream television shows but have now found themselves back in the independents.

Older wrestlers wrap up their careers, doing sometimes decade-long glorified farewell tours.

Then there are those who go back to the indies to touch-up their skills, hone in on their craft, find a new character, or just wait it out until their potential is once again noticed by those who make the big decisions.

The WWE still scouts independents, but now these independent wrestlers, along with athletes and other performers, are brought into their own minor league system and training.

They will work their way into NXT and then up to RAW or Smackdown.

Essentially, you must become a big fish in a small pond and then a bigger pond and then eventually the ocean.

But this does not mean independents don't exist.

101 REASONS TO LOVE PRO WRESTLING

They certainly do.

Whether it's on the way up or on the way down, there is a magic to independent wrestling.

It's a chance to drive down the street to escape into a magical world of performers who are doing what they do out of genuine love for professional wrestling.

If it's 1000 people at a small auditorium or 15 people at a car lot, these wrestlers are living their WrestleMania dreams every cheer, every T-shirt sold, and with ever photo taken.

In baseball they talk about "for the love of the game".

In wrestling there's no bigger love for this crazy world than independent wrestling.

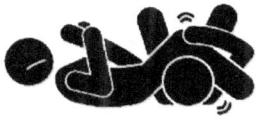

63. SUBMISSION HOLDS

The roots of wrestling go back to ancient Egyptian and Greek cave drawings and artwork.

Grappling is embedded in our history.

It would serve as the highlighted competition of ancient Olympic Games.

In life, we know the pain as an older sibling or school bully making you say "uncle" as they torture you with a noogie and headlock.

It's a test of strength and a display of dominance.

And while Greco-Roman wrestling is still a respected Olympic competition, it is not exactly the same as professional wrestling.

Two wrestlers face off in a physical war with the goal of outlasting and defeating their opponent.

This happens by applying submission holds.

Since the earliest days of professional wrestling the idea of making an opponent submit was the only way to claim victory.

The wrestler grabs an arm, a leg, a neck, or a combination of limbs and stretches their opponent causing excruciating pain.

They stretch. And they stretch.

The tangled wrestler is left with only a few choices.

Tap out or verbally give up, pass out, or escape.

Gory Guerrero invented the la de a caballo.

Which would more commonly be known as, thanks to The Sheik, as the Camel Clutch.

There are basic moves from Greco Roman wrestling that are still successfully used like Bobby Lashley with his vicious Full Nelson.

There are multiple moves that involve attacking the legs like the Figure Four, a leg lock known by millions thanks to "The Nature Boy" Ric Flair.

Then attacking the back and legs with any of the variations of the Boston Crab or Bret "The Hitman" Hart's finishing move, "The Sharpshooter".

It goes on and on and looks increasingly painful and increasingly creative.

And then there's the more unorthodox moves like Mick Foley's Mandible Claw or Killer Kowalski's Stomach Claw.

In today's landscape of wrestling, we are more accustomed to seeing strikes and aerial attacks.

But even now, submission holds are still part of the foundation of the art form.

The classic submissions holds are still around, but are rarely a finishing move.

Then some wrestlers still utilize the tool that is a great submission hold finisher.

At the heart of professional wrestling, there is always going to be point where a wrestler will grab a limb and stretch it.

101 REASONS TO LOVE PRO WRESTLING

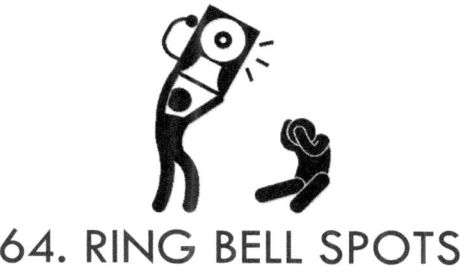

64. RING BELL SPOTS

In a battle it is not uncommon to utilize the element you are in.

When you are in the playground, a hand full of dirt is always there to throw.

When you are in the business world, you use corporate maneuvers to move up the ladder.

When you fight in space, you use space lasers.

It can even be tactical as it is in sports.

Boxers and fighters use the ropes and cage to gain the advantage.

In professional wrestling, utilizing one's element isn't always to gain the upper hand.

Sometimes it is to flat out cheat.

But it's always an act of survival.

There are various items at ringside that a wrestler could use.

Of course, there are chairs, tables, and the randomness under the ring.

But then there's the ring bell.

The device that is used to signify the start of a match, the end of a match, and used in ten bell salutes for fallen heroes.

Simple and to the point.

A wrestler goes outside the ring, takes the ring bell, and then institutes it into the match as a weapon.

It doesn't happen often.

The big blow to the head is a big deal, there is the option to tease, and even the option of ringing it in someone's ear.

It's always a delight to see someone get their bell rung.

101 REASONS TO LOVE PRO WRESTLING

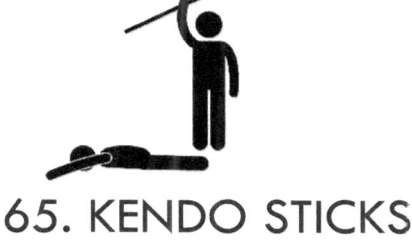

65. KENDO STICKS

The evolution of weaponry has gone from interesting and practical to obscene and unneeded.

During the lineage of the tools of war, some things just stick around.

There are still those who practice archery, while we've moved on to automatic rifles and mistle launchers.

We still use fire and heat in war.

Still, you don't want to show up to a gun fight wielding a knife.

Sometimes a weapon sticks around just because it honors an antiquated past.

The Singapore cane is one of them.

In Singapore, caning is a form of corporal punishment.

Introduced to Singapore by the British in the 19th century, it's a tradition that has stuck around to modern day.

When someone commits a crime, a form of punishment their government will dish out is whacking people with canes.

The cane is known as a rattan, a specific wood that is about a half inch thick and soaked in water overnight to make it supple and to prevent splintering.

But don't worry, they use a smaller cane when caning juveniles.

So, there's that.

101 REASONS TO LOVE PRO WRESTLING

In 1994, an 18-year-old American was convicted of vandalism while visiting.

This would make the news, as the teen would end up receiving four lashes.

And if it's in the news, professional wrestling is listening.

Paul Heyman's Extreme Championship Wrestling was building steam.

It was known as being the brash, vulgar, and hardcore wrestling promotion that is still decades ahead of its time.

While certain "Attitudes" and the extreme styles were adopted from the company, the lightening that was captured in the bottle has not been duplicated.

With his finger on the pulse, Heyman would introduce the Singapore Cane into professional wrestling.

During the same year, Sandman and Tommy Dreamer would compete in a Singapore Cane Match. The loser would receive ten lashes from the came from the victor.

In this career defining moment, Tommy Dreamer took the ten whacks.

Each more painful, with more tears welling up in his eyes, he asks Sandman for another after another.

This dramatic presentation of extreme endurance would change things forever.

The cane used was not the single piece of wood, it would actually be a kendo stick.

A kendo stick is multiple pieces of bamboo put together to form one cane.

The crack of it hurts, but it's nothing in comparison to the stick from Singapore.

Still the reputation is not that much better.

The cane would become a signature for the likes of Sandman and later Justin Credible.

There would be Singapore Cane Matches where the wrestlers would be provided numerous canes to use in their match.

As time would go on, the Singapore cane would just be referred to as what it was, the Kendo Stick.

Like the ladder, chair, and table, the Kendo Stick would just become part of wrestling as in we just accept them to be there and to be used.

It's under the ring for some reason. Chairs and tables are needed furniture items. Tools, Ladders, and even fire extinguishers make sense to be under the ring.

But what is the practical use of there being a kendo stick under the ring?

There is no other use but to grab it, approach your opponent, and swing away.

101 REASONS TO LOVE PRO WRESTLING

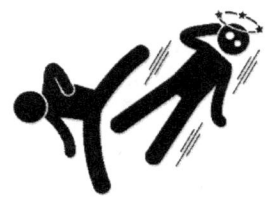

66. FINISHING MOVES

It's that climax with extra oomph that is truly rewarding.

A well-planned meal has a dessert.

Many well composed songs have that big ending.

Everything has an apex. A well fought fight has a final blow. Anything theatrical has an ending.

Professional wrestling has both the final blow and theatrical ending that leave fans in joyous awe.

More times than not, the ending of a match is often preceded by a finishing move.

There are a few different types of finishing moves in professional wrestling.

There are those who utilize a submission move to make their opponent submit via verbally giving up, tapping out, or even passing out.

Long before Ric Flair's "Figure Four" or Bret Hart's "Sharpshooter", old time wrestlers would use leg locks, neck locks, or just flat out bear hugs to take their opponent out.

There are finishing moves that require a set up that tend to crown many champions like a "Jackknife Powerbomb" from Kevin Nash or a "Tombstone Piledriver" from the Undertaker.

Some finishing moves just come out of nowhere.

When you bring up finishing moves out of nowhere it is impossible not to mention Randy Orton's "RKO".

But there is also the "Stone Cold Stunner" from Steve Austin or a simple surprise strike in the likes of a big knockout blow through a monstrous punch from Big Show or a super kick from Shawn Michaels.

The final finishing move type is a crashing splash onto your opponent.

In the most basic form, this is when a bigger wrestler using their weight and gravity to take out their foe.

Hulk Hogan would jump up and drop leg drops to create many iconic moments.

Earthquake would squish opponents and even a snake.

The legendary Yokozuna flattened opponents with his signature "Banzai Drop".

Then those will splash from the top rope. Whether it's an elbow drop from Randy Savage or a big splash from "Superfly" Jimmy Snuka these moves were staples of the 1980's.

Then with the rise of lucha libre and the influence of Japanese light weights, professional wrestling saw its athletes take to the air for some of the most awe-striking finishing moves.

Eddie Guerrero or Rob Van Dam or even D-Lo Brown dropping their version of a frog splash.

This would include the Shooting Star Press from Billy Kidman. A picture perfect moonsault from the Blue Meanie. Maybe a swanton bomb from Jeff Hardy. Or a 450 Splash from AJ Styles.

It does not matter what it is.

If it works, it works.

If the move brings the audience to their feet, stops their heart while pausing time, and widens the eyes of every spectator then it's a success and there is definite victory.

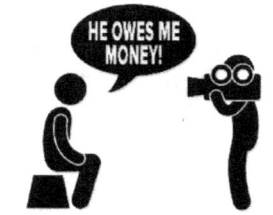

67. SHOOT INTERVIEWS

We like being behind the curtain and velvet rope.

Having knowledge on how something is made or being behind the scenes is appealing to a lot of people.

Interviews have become a staple in all forms of media over the years.

Knowledge is power.

That power comes in many forms.

People just like useless information.

There are those who want to know everything they can about everything they want to know it about.

We dive deep into the ponds that appeal to us.

Sport fans know stats from decades past.

Movie fans know about what happened behind the camera.

Political fans know what really happened and keep tabs on what's going on at the very moment.

The power of knowing all about a beloved topic has become as common as a game show that rewards it.

This is thanks to the sharing of information, and if people want it, it's there.

The world of politics, sports, and entertainment have become 24/7 news fodder.

Professional wrestling provides all three in the same 24/7-time frame.

The reveal about professional wrestling being predetermined was exposed in newspapers going back to the mid-1980's.

From that point the protected Kayfabe of wrestling has been exposed.

There would be exposés on news shows that would expose the business.

There was even a special called "Exposed! Pro Wrestling's Greatest Secrets" that aired on NBC in prime time during the late 1990's.

The idea that professional wrestling is not a legit fight is nothing unheard of. Everyone knows what it is.

Super fans want to know everything that is going on, so being exposed to the inner workings of pro wrestling has become part of the fun.

And where there is a demand, there is a supply.

In the 1990's tape trading craze fans across the globe traded matches and shows with other fans via VHS, so after a few weeks of waiting for the mail, you could be caught up with a market outside of your own.

This was the perfect avenue for small production companies to sit a wrestler down for a candid tell-all interview and then sell it on mass produced VHS tapes.

Companies like Highspots, RF Video, SmartMark Video, and later Kayfabe Commentaries would film performers on their way up, their way down, or in between.

They would go deep on backstage decisions, crazy road stories, and dish the dirt on their experience in the business.

These were the connection to wrestlers that diehard fans yearned for.

It would not be unthinkable to think that a million tapes were traded, passed on, or sold.

Then the internet happened.

Like any artistic medium, downloading became an issue and the common form of trade would become digital.

Then the podcast happened.

A new avenue of verbal destruction was given to the world.

A wrestler will now give their shoot interviews through audio or video podcasts.

It's the same concept as the shoot interviews of the 90's.

Backstage stories are shared, wars of words are had, bridges are burnt, and the view behind the curtain is opened a little more.

And the beauty of the internet is that a shoot interview can be had directly after a news item breaks.

Thanks to shoot interviews we've gone so far behind the curtain that there is absolutely no looking back.

101 REASONS TO LOVE PRO WRESTLING

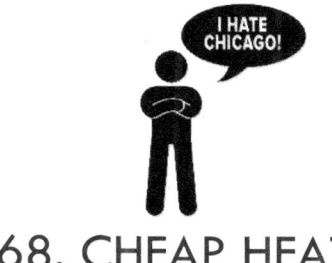

68. CHEAP HEAT

We live in a world full of cliches and stereotypes.

Certain rituals strike a common nerve.

With this, performers, speakers, and just about everyone keeps these tropes up their sleeves.

It could be taking a bow to cue to audience to applaud.

Or it could be making a silly face at a baby for a giggle.

And there is also the alternative... a negative response.

You take the unpopular opinion or find the easiest way to antagonize.

It does not have to be a verbalized attack.

Even when they say "sticks and stones may break my bones, but words will never hurt me" we, the human race, came up with gestures.

If there is an easy way to manipulate a reaction, professional wrestling is going to be there.

Professional wrestling's foundation is built on recycled tropes.

Fans will pop, or cheer, for the good guy, but when a bad guy goes for a negative reaction, it's getting heat.

The simplest of this is cheap heat.

In the older days, and even now, overly patriotic crowds will boo a mean foreign wrestler.

One doesn't have to only rely on jingoistic crowds for cheap heat.

It's yelling at children on their way to the ring.

It's ripping up a sign that a fan worked on at home and brought to the show.

It's mocking the local sports team.

It's disrespectful, mean, and crude but it's rarely ever witty or intelligent.

It's doing the simplest and easiest of tasks to poke at the emotional bear that is a professional wrestling crowd.

And if you don't like that, always remember, your town sucks!

101 REASONS TO LOVE PRO WRESTLING

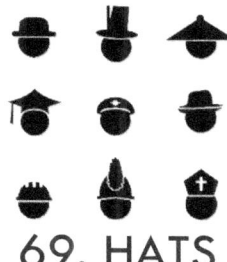

69. HATS

A hat is worn for warmth, religion, or just a fashion accessory.

These head coverings have as deep of a history as any wardrobe option.

Ancient artwork, going back to B.C. times showcases evidence of hats in human culture.

The purposes would evolve over time.

From practical use to status symbols, there have pretty much always been hats worn by many different people.

The warmth and style of head wear is no stranger to the wardrobe of professional wrestling.

In the 1950's, the Australian tag team The Fabulous Kangaroos were famous for wearing slouch hats from their native land.

However, the earliest hats in wrestling would definitely be the crowns worn by kings or cowboy hats worn by, well cowboys.

This tradition would carry on to this day.

The likes of Jerry "The King" Lawler, and just about every winner of the "King of the Ring" tournament, has proudly worn their royal crowns.

As for cowboy hats, the rugged brutes Stan Hansen, Bill Watts, and numerous others have walked to the ring in either a black or white hat.

It doesn't end with the wrestlers. One of the most renowned announcers and personalities in Jim Ross is known for his signature cowboy hat.

There are fedoras, berets, baseball caps, beanies, and many more hat varieties in between.

Professional wrestling is full of characters from all walks of life with their own sense of style.

Of course, they're going to need hats.

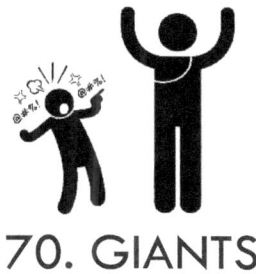

70. GIANTS

All creatures come in different shapes and sizes.

There are hummingbirds, wiener dogs, and goldfish.

But there are also the bigger variations in this.

There are eagles, mastiffs, and whales.

The same goes for humans.

The tallest man in history is Robert Wadlow, standing in at 8 foot 11 inches tall.

While not every giant is as tall as Mr. Wadlow, there are a plethora of examples of giants.

For every Muggsy Bogues or Spud Webb, there is a Shaquille O'Neal or Manute Bol.

The bible even tells us about Goliath while other literature carries on the mythos of giants and larger than life beings.

It doesn't get much larger than life than professional wrestling.

The stature of big men in wrestling goes back to the start of wrestling.

There will always be giants, but Giant Haystacks made a name for himself in the 1970's as being a 6-foot 11 behemoth.

Over the timeline of wrestling there have been plenty of near and surpassing 7-foot stars.

There is Kevin Nash, Kane, the Big Show, Viscera, and the Great Khali to name a few.

All current or future WWE Hall of Famers.

Then there was Giant Gonzales billed at 8 foot tall, Gene Snitsky, Kurgan, and the Yeti.

If one is making a Mount Rushmore of professional wrestling there are a few men that get their own monuments in The Undertaker and of course, the giant of them all, Andre the Giant.

From 1973 to 1991, the eighth wonder of the world Andre the Giant soaked up the jaw dropping, eye widening, and awe-struck responses from millions of wrestling fans.

He is without a doubt the giant of all giants and his legacy is permanent.

There have been many characters in professional wrestling, but if you have to look up... and then even higher than that, then a gigantic impact is made.

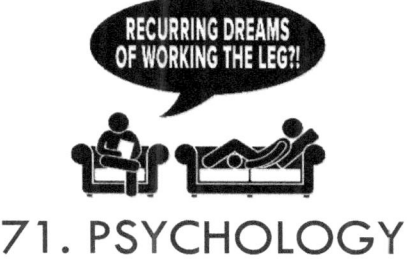

71. PSYCHOLOGY

Psychology is the scientific study of the mind and behavior.

It's been said that 'All we are is dust in the wind'.

Psychology has been a thing we have dealt with since psychiatrists have begun to contemplate the human mind.

We are drawn to certain things. Certain things are "triggers" that affect our emotion. Some things make us happy; some things make us sad, and something pulls us to the edge of our seats in anxious anticipation.

It could be the bottom of the ninth in a suspenseful baseball game. It could be a well written movie that enthralls our attention. It could be any form of emotional manipulation that raises the ire of the audience.

If there is a way to manipulate an audience then professional wrestling is going to pull all the strings possible to sell a character, a match, or story.

In a wrestling match, the objective is to convince the audience what they are seeing is completely real.

That is where psychology comes in.

In professional wrestling, psychology encompassed all of the little things.

It's the little things like working over one body part the whole match to give your finishing move that much more impact.

It's stuff like knowing when to tease a finish just right to get the crowd on the edge of their seats.

To dive deeper would be to reveal literally everything that makes professional wrestling professional wrestling.

Because when it is done right the matches are pure art.

Most fans just watch it and cheer, but most people don't understand they're being manipulated.

It's not just punch, kick, punch, kick.

If you watch the greats or even those who have a grasp on match psychology, then you're set for life.

The match tells a story. How well you tell a story in the ring is what separates wrestlers and legends.

If a finishing move is a submission that hurts the leg, then the obvious psychology is to work over the leg until the big finish.

Psychology is what paints the canvas that is professional wrestling.

Each stroke of paint brings the audience closer and closer to exploding.

Then finally, it's a framed masterpiece.

It's part of history. It's a match that fans will never forget.

It's saying the perfect thing to manipulate the crowd.

It's hitting the perfect move to convince the crowd the near fall they are seeing is going to be the end of the match.

Regardless, psychology is vital.

Yes, it still hurts when you take a bump on the mat, but it hurts even more when the audience is sleeping because you did not tell a convincing story.

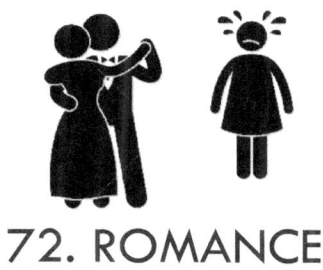

72. ROMANCE

Our society loves a good romance story.

Love is so important that we have a "heart" symbol that doesn't exactly look like a human or animal heart.

Based on the heart-shaped peepal leaves, the heart logo goes back to artistic depictions of the Indus Valley Civilization.

There is speculation that this leaf was used as a contraceptive, which is both ironic and makes perfect sense. We're talking as long ago as the 5th or 6th century B.C.

Over the centuries, the use of the symbol would develop and by the 16th century in Europe the heart symbol as we know it would become a visual staple.

In so many words, we love to love.

Readers, viewers, and super fans all indulge the fantasy of two people connecting, igniting passion, and falling in love.

Be it Romeo and Juliet, Bonnie and Clyde, or even Spiderman and Mary Jane, there are many stories to tickle that sentimental urge.

They say, "love is in the air" and professional wrestling definitely breathes that very same air.

The most memorable and heralded romance in professional wrestling is undoubtedly "Macho Man" Randy Savage and Miss Elizabeth.

In reality, they would be married for a handful of years and would break up with a lot of drama attached.

But in the world of wrestling, these two were THEE couple in the 80's.

From heel to face, this relationship was part of one of the biggest eras of the industry.

Their conflicts are part of history.

Their reunion and wedding brought tears.

There would also be the unexpected romances.

Spike Dudley and Molly Holly.

Otis and Mandy Rose.

Mark Henry and Mae Young.

It goes on and on and includes the likes of Hall of Famers like Chyna and Eddy Guerrero.

Then real life meets the screen when a behind the scenes relationship becomes an on-screen story.

Everyone knows the backstage politics and workings, so it's only natural that real life relationships become part of the story.

With this comes the Stephanie McMahon and Triple H relationship.

There's the awkward situation with Edge, Matt Hardy, and Lita.

If there is anything that can add fuel to the fire of a story, it's a war of love.

And of course, there is just something magical about weddings in professional wrestling.

The Nielson ratings have proven that weddings on wrestling shows are not only memorable, but also a big hit.

Of course, we had the aforementioned "Macho Man" and Miss Elizabeth wedding, but there's more and more that sparks memories in the mind of every long-time wrestling fan.

101 REASONS TO LOVE PRO WRESTLING

We've seen Triple H marry a passed-out Stephanie McMahon in a drive-thru Vegas wedding.

We've seen the most bizarre of bizarre weddings in Lita marrying Kane.

We've even seen heart attacks in the form of Torrie Wilson's father.

We professional wrestling fans love our wrestling weddings.

If love didn't matter to wrestling there wouldn't be a Brother Love, Angelina Love, or Dude Love. Or any of the Love family.

In a world of brutes that battle it out over championship belts and grudges, sometimes it's a refreshing change of pace to see a romance story fill up the many hours of weekly television.

There is nothing that can't be sealed with a kiss.

101 REASONS TO LOVE PRO WRESTLING

73. ACTION FIGURES

For centuries statues were erected for highly regarded people.

For many of those centuries, children played with dolls.

This could be a baby doll, a puppet, or anything one could played with or enjoyed by a child.

As commerce boomed in the 1900's, toys became a huge industry.

In 1959, Mattel introduced Barbie. A blonde female doll with fashion accessories and play sets.

The Barbie Doll was aimed towards girls and was a huge success. It would not be long before boys would get their own doll outside of Barbie's boyfriend Ken.

The term "action figure" was coined by Hasbro in 1964 in a marketing effort to sell G.I. Joes as something other than dolls.

From then action figures would be marketed towards boys as a masculine equivalent to dolls.

Of course, we now know kids can play with whatever and no one should care, but the stigma of "boys playing with dolls" would be erased with this marketing front.

Superheroes, sport stars, television characters, and other popular personas would be made into small toy statues for children to use to recreate what they've seen and indulge in an imaginative world.

Professional wrestling, of course, would not miss a chance to add another product to their merchandising.

101 REASONS TO LOVE PRO WRESTLING

Wrestling action figures actually go back to the 1969 Bullmark series where the Japan Pro Wrestling Alliance released small plastic figures of international legends like Antonia Inoki and Giant Baba among others.

Then in 1981, the company called POPY released a set of wrestling action figures as well.

Still, the story of professional wrestling action figures must be told through the eyes of a life-long WWF fan.

In 1984 WWF would sign on with the company LJN. The WWF Wrestling Superstars series would be launched.

Standing in at eight inches tall, each superstar came with a biography card on the outside packaging and included a poster inside.

The consumer was definitely getting their money's worth as these non-poseable rubber figures would rule the land.

LJN would provide us with 6 single series and 1 set of tag team box sets featuring the likes of Hulk Hogan, Andre the Giant, Junkyard Dog, "Rowdy" Roddy Piper, and other icons, the history of professional wrestling figures really begins here.

As of 2021, LJN figures would still be a collectors dream as some rare figures, prototypes, and unique variations.

After LJN's contract ended and the company was sold, the WWF would have to seek another company to produce their figures.

Enter Hasbro.

From 1990 to 1994, Hasbro would produce ELEVEN different series of figures and various rings and tag team packages.

Made up of mostly hard plastic, these four-inch figures would finally have some articulation in the form of spring-loaded signature moves like big punches, clotheslines, drop kicks, and slams.

Each figure would again include a biography card on the back of the package, but no posters this time.

183

When they are cranking out ELEVEN series in less than five years, there is no time for posters.

Hasbro would have the same icons of the 80's as LJN in Hulk Hogan, Andre the Giant, "Macho Man", and others.

However, they would also introduce the first figures for the likes of Shawn Michaels, Razor Ramon, Mr. Perfect, I.R.S., Owen Hart, 1-2-3 Kid, and Yokozuna among many other future legends.

Hasbro collectors will pay top dollar to relive their childhoods and hoard mint on card figures as well as any weird variant they can get.

Some have paid upwards of $15,000 and more to be able to claim ownership for figures as obscure as a Rhythm and Blues, black haired version of Greg Valentine.

This is just one crazy example of other crazy dealings, all over action figures.

Let's not even get into the "moon on belly" version of the Hasbro Kamala.

From 1994 to 1996, professional wrestling fans felt a void of no company making action figures.

Thankfully, in 96 Jakks Pacific made the run-in. From 1996 until December of 2009, Jakks would capitalize on the Attitude Era.

With numerous series of the "Superstars" line and then a ton of other series, Jakks made plenty of wrestling fans happy with "Bone Crunching Action" and more articulation than has been seen or played with before.

With Jakks we'd get the first "Stone Cold" Steve Austin, the first Rock, first Mankind, and first of many legends.

Over this twelve plus year relationship, Jakks released other sets including the STOMP series, Signature Series, and then the Ruthless Aggression set.

Ruthless Aggression would feature 15 points of articulation and would be considered Jakks most successful line.

101 REASONS TO LOVE PRO WRESTLING

The innovations did not end there. The inclusion of the WWE Classic Superstars line would showcase legends, alumni, and heroes from the past.

Then on January 1st, 2010, wwe.com would announce a new line of figures with a new company, Mattel.

During the ongoing decade of innovation, Mattel has created hundreds of WWE action figures.

We've seen Entrance Greats, Legends, and the awe-striking Elite series.

The same size as Jakks, but a whole lot more detailed these action figures brought, and as of now, continue to bring the action.

In 2019, Mattel launched their Ultimate series. These ongoing set showcases the biggest stars with the most options for posing. Often including multiple heads with multiple expressions, different hand poses, and a plethora of accessories.

The innovation continues to this day making fans and collectors excited with every new announcement.

Outside of the WWE lineage, professional wrestling action figures have been put out by other companies.

In 85, AWA would team up with REMCO for smaller sized figures. These two packs saw Greg Gagne and Jim Brunzell, Steve Keirn and Stan Lane, and the ever so awesome duo of Larry Zbyszko and Ric Flair.

In 1990 WCW released rubber twistables showcasing their biggest stars at the time like Sid Vicious, the Steiner Brothers, and of course "Nature Boy" Ric Flair.

Then in the same year of 90, GALOOB would drop their own line of WCW figures.

A blink of an eye later in 1995, Original San Francisco Toy Makers would also team up with WCW for LJN-comparable pieces of rubber.

These big clunky figures would not be posable.

Then in 1998, Original San Francisco Toy Makers would drop slightly more posable figures around the time nWo and crow-Sting were tearing up the Nielson ratings.

The same company would release figures for ECW in 1999. This awesome line-up had all the ECW greats from "The Franchise" Shane Douglas, New Jack, Sabu, Rob Van Dam, and others extreme icons.

In 99, TOY BIZ released what would have been WCW's last line. This set was by far the most detailed of the WCW run and had articulation comparable to what would be WWE's run with Mattel. A set WAY before it's time.

Outside of WCW and ECW, wrestling figures would exist from other companies. The 2005 Marvel line of TNA Impact figures existed. They weren't exactly selling out, but somewhere very nice figures.

Outside of dollar store knock offs, the wrestling figure scene would be desolate unless living in the WWE timeline.

That was until 2020 when JAZWARES connected with All Elite Wrestling.

These AEW figures are on par with the best of what Mattel has put out for the WWE, but features the likes of Orange Cassidy, Darby Allin, Jungle Boy, MJF, and the rest of the star-studded roster.

There does not look to be an end to this relationship.

Anyone who grew up with wrestling would have a hard time not strolling the toy aisle and checking out the figures.

There are websites delving deep into the world of wrestling figures.

There are podcasts that cover past, present, and future action figures. Some of these podcasts even involve life-long fans who happen to also have figures made of themselves.

Yes, even the wrestlers themselves can be fans of wrestling toys. People collect everything they can if it has either financial or emotional value. Professional wrestling toys provide both.

What was a chance to escape as a child, is a chance to reflect on great times as an adult collector.

Whether you buy the figures to open or "let them breath" as former WrestleMania winners say, or keeping them mint on card, a collection means a lot to a fan if it's a $15,000 prototype or a $5 discount bin dust collector.

At the end of the day, the dream is always alive in the form of action figures.

101 REASONS TO LOVE PRO WRESTLING

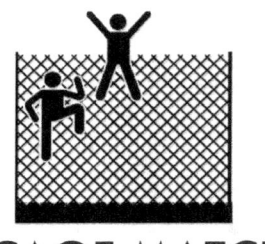

74. CAGE MATCHES

Captivity comes in many forms.

The idea of a cage goes back as far as practical has been practical.

A cage is used to contain life stock, and also a prison to keep bad people away from the general public.

It's also used for cage fighting.

In professional wrestling, the cage should be looked at from three perspectives: Structure, Booking, and the Legacy.

The structure of a cage in professional wrestling varies.

NWA, WCW, ECW, and later WWE would use the normal cage. A chain linked fence connected by steel pipes.

This is the tradition, the standard if you will, of a cage in professional wrestling.

The old school WWF cage was an awesome blue barred nightmare.

It was a big metal structure with big open spaces between bars and left fans of that time with many great memories.

Various companies have adopted the War Games style match. Two rings and one gigantic cage around the entire monstrosity. These matches have been historic and the excellence in the art of violence.

The booking of a Cage Match is simple.

It draws, and when something draws it means more money is made.

It's often used as the culmination of a big money feud that needs a big blow off match that will sell the tickets, the pay per views, and be the end-all in anticipation of closure between two rivals that despise one another.

It could be because a bad guy keeps trying to get away or having outside forces interfere and THIS is the only way to keep a fight uncontested.

Or it be two wrestlers that hate each other so much that something barbaric is needed to finally settle the score.

Regardless, it draws.

It's a gimmick that the storytellers use to raise eyebrows, get excited, and spend their hard-earned money.

That doesn't mean there isn't an art to the Cage Match.

The legacy of a Cage Match in professional wrestling goes back to the late 30's in Atlanta, Georgia where Jack Bloomfield and Count Pietro Rossi fought in a ring surrounded by chicken wire.

The traditional steel cage would come in 1942 at an Ontario, Canada show that saw John Katan defeat Ignacio Martinez.

This would evolve and become a featured attraction across the territories.

By the mid-70's, Bruno Sammartino was taking on Lou Albano in a Cage Match for the WWF World Title and Wahoo McDaniel was taking on Ric Flair in a cage match of their own.

By this point, it would always be an ace up any matchmakers sleeve to use to make a match just that much more special.

The quality of the Cage Matches would vary, but there have been many great matches and memorable moments over the decades past.

A moment that is instilled into the minds of older fans and fans of Mick Foley is when Jimmy Snuka dove off the top of a cage at a WWF MSG show.

There was also Starrcade 83 that saw Ric Flair defeat Harley Race.

For many longtime fans, the NWA Starrcade 85 "I Quit" Cage Match comes to mind when discussing this gimmick match. Magnum TA would defeat Tully Blanchard by attempting to stab his opponent in the eye with the leg of broken chair.

Bret Hart and Owen Hart stole the show at Summer Slam 1994.

"Stone Cold" Steve Austin and Vince McMahon even had a memorable Cage Match at St. Valentine Day's Massacre.

Hell in a Cell would see the likes of Shawn Michaels and Undertaker define the match and then Undertaker and Mankind redefine it with some of the most memorable moments in professional wrestling.

The two-ring caged War Games was done first in NWA, but NXT, MLW, AEW, and then GCW have all done their own version.

Tag teams would also have their moments in the cage as well with the likes of the Dudleys and Hardyz at Survivor Series 2001 or even Young Bucks defeating the Lucha Brothers at All Out 2021.

And that's just a few legendary matches that have taken place inside of an unforgiving steel structure.

It goes on and on.

A Cage Match can even make the not-so-good at least "okay" or "watchable".

It's a Cage Match! It's always worth stopping for a moment and checking out.

It's the "in the moment" excitement and the big spots that make these matches so special.

The ones where they end with someone climbing over and escaping are fun.

101 REASONS TO LOVE PRO WRESTLING

The extra feat adds to the anticipation.

The classic Cage Match, however, is sold as "no one can enter, no one can leave" and it's a great spectacle or brutality.

It ends when someone gives up or is a pinned.

Regardless, it would be hard to imagine professional wrestling without the signature Cage Match.

As the owner of the NWA once sang, 'despite of my rage, I'm still just a rat in a cage."

101 REASONS TO LOVE PRO WRESTLING

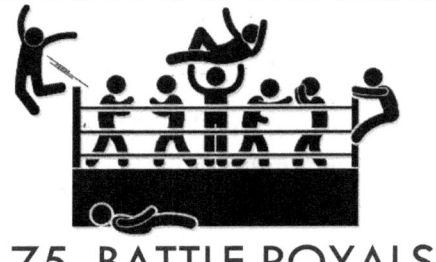

75. BATTLE ROYALS

Combat sports have been around for millenniums.

The battle royal goes back many centuries.

It's as simple as putting a few people in one space and let them go at it until there is one last person standing.

Sadly, this includes slave fights in the early 18th century where barbaric and horrible people were barbaric and horrible.

This should be noted, but battle royals how we know them today are much more innocent and is pretty much just another match type.

It was also originally a fight between multiple boxers.

They'd abide by the rules of boxing, but in essence, it was fisticuffs in the form of a free for all.

This was often the opening bout for wrestling and boxing shows from around the 1870's until about 1910.

It would still linger in some areas but would eventually fade out in the 1950's.

It's a big spectacle and a big brawl. So of course, professional wrestling would adopt it.

The idea of a battle royal in wrestling goes back to "Toots" Mondt, a member of the Gold Dust Trio, the ground breakers of what professional wrestling would become.

101 REASONS TO LOVE PRO WRESTLING

"Toots" took the boxing fight gimmick and put his own spin on it for the world of professional wrestling.

A battle royal in professional wrestling does not involve gloves.

It typically involves from a dozen to dozens of wrestlers fighting it out in a ring.

Then the object is to toss everyone over the top rope with their feet hitting the ground.

Rinse and repeat until there is one wrestler left. The victor.

The chaos of a ring full of wrestlers trying to be the sole winner of such a crazy match is as exciting as anything professional wrestling can visually provide.

It would be a staple in wrestling across all modern eras.

Then in 1988, the World Wrestling Federation introduced the Royal Rumble.

The Royal Rumble is the most famous of the battle royals. Until this point, all the wrestlers would enter the ring before the match started.

However, the Royal Rumble would use a random drawing gauntlet format that added another level of anticipation and surprise.

The winner would ceremoniously receive a shot at the World Title at Wrestle Mania, making it a highly sought-after feat.

Mostly all companies eventually have a battle royal on their card, but some companies have put their own spin on it as WWF did with the Rumble.

WCW would have the Lethal Lottery Battle Bowl that saw the winners of a series of randomly drawn tag team matches all entered the main event battle bowl to win a fancy ring.

While fun, it wasn't as big as the Royal Rumble.

So, they tried to outdo it with mass in the terms of a World War 3 battle royal with 60 men in three rings.

All Elite Wrestling has their own spin on the traditional battle royal with their Casino Battle Royal.

It's the same concept as the Royal Rumble but it's not a one-by-one entrance. It's broken down into groupings with one final "Joker" card entering at the end.

Major League Wrestling has their "Battle Riot" which uses the Rumble rules as well, but their spin is that eliminations happen via pinfall, submission, and being thrown over the top rope.

Whether the competitors enter every minute or so, or the competitors are all piled into the ring at the start of the match, battle royals are always fun to see.

If there's enough variety in styles, a battle royal can be a virtual buffet of brutality.

There are the standards that every good battle royal has.

It's unlikely allies teaming up to get out a bigger wrestler.

It's likely allies tossing each other out in their pursuit of solo glory.

Then there's the teases where someone, somehow and someway, does NOT get eliminated.

It could be someone catches you and puts back in the ring. This is an act often used by bad guys but has also seen its share of good guys using the tactic.

There's showcases of jaw dropping athleticism like when Shawn Michaels would pull himself back into the ring with a move dubbed "skinning the cat", which was essentially a 360 degree pull up from the hanging off ropes to being back to your feet in the ring.

Others have combined this display of physicality with a display of creativity as Kofi Kingston has done in multiple situations. He has done many outrageous and awesome things to ensure his feet did not touch the ground.

Winning a battle royal can sometimes win someone a championship, make them a contender, or just provides a big stake bragging right.

As the anticipation builds the crowd cheers, the crowd boos, tensions are tested, and the audience is taken on a roller coaster of emotions from the sounding of the ring bell until the final feet hit the floor.

101 REASONS TO LOVE PRO WRESTLING

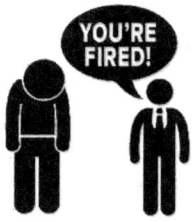

76. AUTHORITY FIGURES

No one wants to be told what to do.

The everyday man has everyday bosses. These bosses give us assignments, things that need to be done, and the majority are unlikable.

In professional wrestling it is very rare that an authority figure is a kindhearted person.

They are portrayed as vindictive, mean, and downright evil.

However, we still have authority figures in our lives who tell us what to do.

The traditional family unit has parents that tell children how to live their lives as they grow up.

While we grow up, we experience many others that dictate our fates.

There is the law that governs the land. There are teachers that assign us homework. We have officials in sports to uphold the rules of the game. And for many, there are religious deities that we set our moral compasses to.

Then we do grow up. We can start making our own decisions.

Except we must work, so we have bosses.

Like Huey Lewis's angelic voice tells us, we're all 'workin' for a livin'.

Our bosses control our focus for sometimes forty plus hours a week.

Sometimes we get fed up and quit these jobs, but most of the time we accept our place as a cog in the wheel and just do what we have to do.

101 REASONS TO LOVE PRO WRESTLING

It's a status that we all have to deal with. A common man issue that many people feel very strongly about.

So of course, professional wrestling would delve into these emotions and present their own authority figures.

There have been a large variety of authority figures in wrestling of different types.

In the early days of wrestling, the authority figure would be the commissioner or president of the company. They would step in and make matches, break up fights, hand out fines, and put their foot down when things got too heated.

The NWA would rely on a "Championship Committee" to make the decisions on big matches.

With this, in NWA and later WCW and TNA, there would be a representative of the committee in the form of legends like Dusty Rhodes and Larry Zbyszko.

There would be Eric Bischoff running WCW and then Dixie Carter running TNA Impact.

Pretty much every smaller company since, from Paul Heyman and ECW to a random guy at your random local independent, has had its own form of authority figure.

There would be many notable figures and beloved characters, but no one really nailed the performance of this role quite like the WWE.

The WWWF, WWF, and later the WWE would always uphold someone to the highest position. From its founding in 1963 all the way until 1997, the president ruled the show.

The World Wrestling Federation would feature Jack Tunney, a long time Canadian promoter and performer, that would suspend those who got too vicious, announce big matches, and in the case of the Royal Rumble in 1994, would make the big decision to hold a coin toss between the two winners of the match.

This would evolve to others like Gorilla Monsoon and then Sargent Slaughter as those who would have to lay down the law.

As the 90's progressed, these figures would become more and more part of the story lines.

This would eventually blow-up when Vince McMahon would begin to showcase his known real-life authority on camera with a heinous Mr. McMahon character.

When you have a personality as big as Mr. McMahon you would need a foil for him. "Stone Cold" Steve Austin would become the natural choice for this endeavor.

Some of the most entertaining moments of the Attitude Era saw the "Tom and Jerry"-like war between McMahon and the "Texas Rattlesnake".

If all good things come to an end, it would be inevitable that a great feud like this would also come to pass.

However, the authority figure persona would remain.

Iconic wrestlers like Shawn Michaels, Mick Foley, William Regal, and others would take on roles as the commissioner.

Then the role would change to be "General Managers". With the WWE splitting their roster between two shows, each presentation would have an authority figure to ensure the inmates never ran the asylum.

If there was a brawl between multiple wrestlers, it would be expected for Teddy Long to come out and book a Tag Team Match.

Or, if you were being a real pest, he'd book you to go one on one with the Undertaker to set you right.

It goes on and on.

There was even a period in WWE where a ringside laptop would run the show and make the big decisions.

101 REASONS TO LOVE PRO WRESTLING

There is nothing like getting off school, clocking out from work, or just kicking back after a long day than watching the professional wrestling escapism that is raging against the machine.

Being able to live out our disruptive dreams in the scenario of speaking up for yourself, taking your fate into your own hands, or just beating up those who have told you "No" is a precious gift.

We really do not like being told what to do. So why would our professional wrestling heroes?

As "Stone Cold" Steve Austin proved in all his glory, you don't have to take it.

You just kick your employer in the gut, drop them with a "Stone Cold" Stunner, and celebrate with copious amounts of beer.

101 REASONS TO LOVE PRO WRESTLING

77. OBVIOUS DISTRACTIONS

We are all suckers for some kind of illusion.

Some of us are put in awe from the sight of a magic trick.

A lot of us fall for the illusion of love only seen in trashy romance novels.

There is a big chunk of the masses who believe in a magical being controlling our existence.

Ghosts are real, Aliens are among us, and if you ask some people, the Earth itself is flat.

And of course... Magnets. How do those work?

There is a logical answer to everything, but for whatever reason, we mentally block logic on some things and just let ourselves get caught up in the magic.

We benefit from the escapism while the performer or source benefits from pulling it off convincingly.

In professional wrestling, falling for the trick often results in defeat or looking like a fool.

There are some weird aspects about professional wrestling that people just accept for no reason.

And stupid reasons where a wrestler is so easily distracted is a common recurring trope.

And these scenarios are lame.

Wrestler A is in the ring for a match and Wrestler B's music hits distracting Wrestler A long enough for whoever his opponent is to roll them up and pin them or attack them.

It's not JUST music.

Wrestler B can just walk out and get attention. Wrestler A automatically forgets that he's in a match and in a fight so he can scowl and shake fists at someone.

There is always the sneak attack.

Wrestler A is in the ring, Wrestler B's entrance music hits and Wrestler A turns their attention to the entrance way. Then Wrestler B enters from behind and attacks stupid Wrestler A.

Wrestler A hits a big move that takes out Wrestler B. It seems legit, the medical staff enters the ring, and they are legitimately hurt.... or so we think.

Then there's the ol' Eddie Guerrero trick.

Eddie gets the referee to look away, tosses Wrestler A a chair, falls like Wrestler A hit him with the chair with the anticipation of Wrestler A getting called for the Disqualification.

All in all, Wrestler A is pretty stupid.

Yes, we still cheer them on. We still want to see them get their comeuppance. We still allow the excitement of them winning a big match make or break our day.

And of course, we still jump from the edge of our seats and shouting, "Quick! Look behind you!"

101 REASONS TO LOVE PRO WRESTLING

78. MASKS

Art has dictated the term "mask" as a face without a body.

The many forms of masquerade go back to the B.C. times, where masks were made of stone.

However, the true invention and origins remains an anthropological mystery.

Over multiple millennia, many cultures would adopt their own masked rituals.

It's an imaginative experience that has played a vital part in the history of humanity.

It's more than a mere piece of costume.

A mask serves many purposes.

It could be to withhold one's identity.

It could be for protection.

It could be for ceremony.

In professional wrestling, masks have been used for all these reasons and more.

At the 1865 World's Fair in Paris, Theobaud Bauer introduced the mask to wrestling under the gimmick of "The Masked Wrestler".

Mort Henderson would introduce his gimmick of the "Masked Marvel" in America in 1915.

When talking about masks in wrestling, one must delve into the world of lucha libre.

The history of the lucha libre style of wrestling has roots embedded in acrobatic masked combat.

Mexico is often credited as the originator of masks with hyperbole of mythical ancient roots, but that is not the real story.

After seeing "Cyclone" McKey, an American masked wrestler in Texas, a Mexican promoter would not only bring him to their territory but adopt the mask for a whole new culture of wrestling fans.

The company EMLL would essentially take the mask and run with it.

They created many masked characters showcasing different characters that would become the standard in lucha libre.

The craftsmanship of these masks is a true skill of art and elaborate creativity.

This would lead to a plethora of masked performers who have made a flipping splash in the history of wrestling.

The Villanos, La Parka, El Santo, and others would become world famous for their masks and their skills in the ring.

The prolific Mil Mascaras was so popular in the 1960's and 70's that he would become a cultural icon.

In Mexico, the mask is treated as scared with most masked performers refusing to let their real face ever be shown.

So, if a masked wrestler was being interviewed by media, the mask would remain on. If they were in movies or just doing everyday things in the public, the mask would always remain on.

There have been many luchador performers to wear a mask from the past, present, and future generations but the most famous modern day masked wrestler is without a doubt Rey Mysterio.

Mysterio has held many championship belts and have been involved in many historic moments. Just about all those championships and moments have been while wearing majestic masks.

There have been other performers to wear masks in history as well. A prime example is Mr. Wrestling, Mr. Wrestling II, III, IV, V, and likely even more.

Japan has seen a few generations of Tiger Mask performers.

There was Big Van Vader's "evil jockstrap" mask.

Kane's red leather mask.

Mankind's brown leather mask.

The Fiend's horror-inspired mask is one of the more recent additions to the lore of iconic masks.

There have been the likes of Mortis, Juan Cena, Abyss, Aldo Montoya, The Executioners, The Patriot, and hundreds of others.

It's just another visual to add to the show, but it's not a crutch.

If a wrestler is great, mask or not, then they will be successful.

If someone isn't that great there is no mask that will make them any better.

For many, the true workings of what it takes to create something magical in professional wrestling is never fully understood.

An element like a mask only adds to the mystery.

79. GREAT PROMOS

Speaking with conviction is what riles up the troops, gets people on your side, and helps convince someone of a story being told.

A carnival barker will use inflection and excitement to sell a ticket.

In boxing, greats like Muhammad Ali would showcase a witty and confident attitude in pre-fight interviews that would make people want to buy tickets and tune in.

It is definitely a way to promote so it would only be a logical connection to selling tickets for professional wrestling.

A promo in professional wrestling is a performance within itself.

It's verbally enticing emotion, engaging the crowd, and capturing the energy of those in attendance to give a match-up, or the arching story being told, move life than what would initially be on paper.

The mouthpieces of professional wrestling would notoriously be the managers. Those who would accompany the wrestler to the ring, interact with the audience, and be the vocal representation.

Icons like Paul Heyman, Bobby Heenan, Jim Cornette, The Grand Wizard, and a slew of other managers would grab a microphone and antagonize the audience into hating the bad guy and loving the good guy.

There would also be numerous Hall of Famers who would be able to back up the action in the ring with great promos.

The characters and characterizations of professional wrestling has always been over the top.

101 REASONS TO LOVE PRO WRESTLING

A good performer can display this in the ring with their work, but a great performer can do this both in the ring and behind a microphone.

Some are just naturals. They can get their point across with ease and take the crowd on a journey just with the power of their voice.

It's an art form that those outside of the fandom of wrestling blindly ignore.

Like any superhero or action star, there are one liners that just become super famous.

Hulk Hogan had "Whatcha' Gonna Do…".

"Macho Man" Randy Savage had "Oh Yeah!"

"Stone Cold" Austin has "The Bottom Line".

D-Generation X has "Suck It!".

Bret Hart had his "Best there is, best there was, and best there ever will be".

The Rock has "Do Ya Smell What The Rock is Cookin'?"

Undertaker had "Rest in Peace".

If there is a legend, odds are most of them have their signature slogans to use and rile up the crowd.

In the earliest years, guys like "Superstar" Billy Graham used his persona to push matches.

When you talk to a professional wrestling fan who has either lived through it or done their research, there are a handful of performers who resonate most when it comes to delivering a great promo.

Dusty Rhodes spoke the language of the audience. They related. His promos would be both relatable to the common man while providing hope that right would overcome the wrong.

Ric Flair is known for his "Woos", but his "Nature Boy" persona would shine when a microphone was put in front of him.

Mick Foley has had different characters, but his talent in capturing the attention and touching the souls of those who are watching is a skill sharper than any skill in human existence.

Others like legends like John Cena or icons like Raven, Jake "The Snake" Roberts, and the "Million Dollar Man" Ted DiBiase would be able to verbally play with the audience's collective emotions like a cat toying with a mouse.

Professional wrestling fans love professional wrestling, but it does not end with the action told between the ropes.

Sometimes, you need that extra boost to care, that extra kick in the tail to focus on the story being told, or just that extra slap in the face; all to really get your blood pumping.

A great promo does just that.

101 REASONS TO LOVE PRO WRESTLING

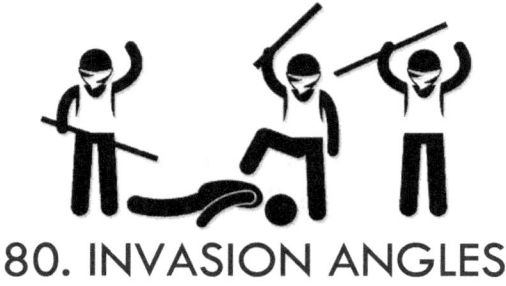

80. INVASION ANGLES

We have been invaded.

An invasion is a military action of soldiers entering a foreign land.

This has the obvious connotations and it's also a term attached to the arts.

Be it a military attack or being overtaken by aliens, the concept of invasion has been and is an active plot line in both real life and beyond.

Our history books are full of real-life examples.

The lineage of performance art is also littered with its own depictions.

Naturally, professional wrestling would also have its own invasion moments littered throughout its history.

During the territory era of wrestling there would always be a revolving door of talents coming and going on their journey.

While one wrestler could technically "invade" a new promotion, an invasion is also technically a military action.

We've had 'One Man Gangs', but a military is never one sole man.

And yes, there would be groups that would arrive to a new area at the same time, but the grandiose moment of invasions would not be as memorable until well into the television area.

In the 80's and 90's there would be invasion moments like Jim Cornette bringing the NWA to WWF or Paul Heyman bringing his ECW to a WWF Monday Night RAW.

Then in the late 90's, professional wrestling fans experienced one of the most unexpected moments. A moment where you suspend all belief and think "this is NOT supposed to happen!"

This would be the New World Order's invasion of WCW.

The initial idea was said to be borrowed from an old story line of the American company UWF invading New Japan Pro Wrestling but the nWo was totally its own thing.

Former WWF stars and detractors from WCW would come together to run amuck for a handful of years that brought WCW it's biggest moments, most money, and for 83 weeks the best television ratings of any professional wrestling show.

There would be other invasions after this. D-Generation X was loosely an invasion stable, but more so just disrupters to the norm.

WWE would try to recreate the magic by having WCW invade once Vince McMahon bought the company.

They would also have Nexus, Retribution, and others enter the scene under the guise of an invasion story line.

Other companies would have invasions of their own. TNA Impact had Aces & Eights invade and Immortal before them.

Ring of Honor would be invaded by independent rivals from CZW.

You watch a company, follow the stories, and invest yourself into the world of wrestling.

Then an invasion shakes things up.

A wall you never knew existed is knocked down and a whole new world of danger and possibility is revealed.

101 REASONS TO LOVE PRO WRESTLING

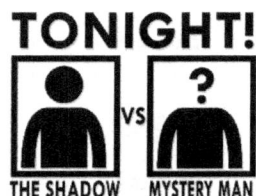

81. MYSTERY OPPONENTS & PARTNERS

Not knowing what's around the corner is always a thrill.

It could be an unwrapped gift. It could be a blind date. It could be walking through your yard with your eyes closed.

In movies, comic books, and the arts there have always been stories a protagonist taking on an unknown foe.

However, an organized fight or sporting event, the fighter, player, or team always goes into their competition knowing who will be on the other side.

Professional wrestling takes the unknown magic of the arts and combines it with the organized competition of a big game.

This is in the form of mystery opponents and partners.

This professional wrestling trope is ultimately about baited anticipation.

It's not knowing who the participants of a match will be.

A match is set. The wrestler enters the ring. Then said wrestler and the audience all wait. The wonder of who will be the next wrestler introduced is anticipated.

Enter the mystery opponent.

The piece of storytelling goes back to the roots of modern wrestling.

A mystery opponent occurs formally as dictated by the company or it can happen organically.

When an established star, be it champion or not, has a standing "open challenge", it is always interesting to see who is going to accept it.

The more recurring storytelling touch point is where the authority figure will have a wrestler face off against someone of their choosing that will be revealed at match time.

One of the most historic mystery opponent moments occurred at Summer Slam in 1988. The Ultimate Warrior's entrance blew the roof off the arena as he showed up to quickly defeat The Honky Tonk Man, and thus win the Intercontinental Championship.

There are some instances where the mystery becomes a regular occurrence.

The Royal Rumble will often reveal all of the competitors, but sometimes they hold back a few to allow for speculation.

The two biggest examples of this would be John Cena making his surprise comeback or Edge returning from years of an injury-related absence.

Then there are surprise debuts in the Royal Rumble like when AJ Styles made his long-awaited arrival in shocking fashion.

All Elite Wrestling has a mystery opponent built into their battle royals as an unknown and unannounced competitor enters as the "Joker Card".

Sometimes there is a lot of hype, that does not exactly live up to the promotion.

This would be the case with The Black Scorpion from WCW in the early 1990's.

It's hit or miss in result, but the execution of the concept is where the magic is.

A mystery partner is exactly how it sounds.

This variation of the idea involves a match that has one tag team taking on one person who has not revealed who would be their partner.

At the Survivor Series in 1990, "The Million Dollar Man" Ted DeBiase introduced his mystery partner in The Undertaker.

Owen Hart would declare he had a mystery partner for his Tag Team Title Match at WrestleMania XI that turned out to be Hall of Famer Yokozuna.

The New World Order would kick off with a Mystery "Third Man" that would be revealed as Hulk Hogan, turning heel on his beloved following.

We also saw Dude Love debut as a mystery partner to "Stone Cold" Steve Austin on an Attitude Era episode of Monday Night RAW.

The same could be said of Sasha Banks' surprise partner in a debuting from NXT Bayley.

Then there were moments like 1996, when Jimmy "Superfly" Snuka was a letdown at his Survivor Series appearance.

Using a mystery partner is also a way to replace someone who is either hurt or cannot make the show.

At No Way Out of Texas in 1998, Shawn Michaels couldn't participate for one night D-Generation X would team up with Savio Vega.

No matter what, the mystery is still there.

The fans never really know who is coming out of that curtain.

If it's a big surprise, then it makes for a magical moment.

If it's a letdown, it's still a moment regardless of magic.

Because whether it be a gasp to the shocker, a sigh of relief, or a groan of disappointment it's that frozen heartbeat that precedes it that truly matters.

101 REASONS TO LOVE PRO WRESTLING

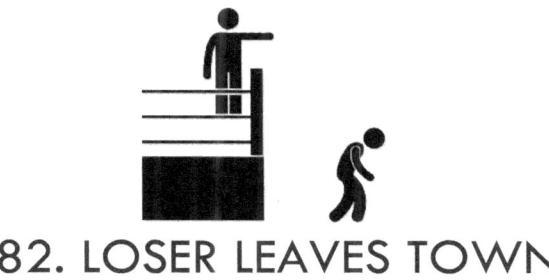

82. LOSER LEAVES TOWN

No one wants to be left out.

We need to be part of a community.

Our society is based on being a part of something greater than yourself.

When that is abruptly taken away, all hope is lost.

Outside of being a social outcast, there are exiled norms in our culture with the two biggest examples being within the law of the land and within the rules of the house.

If you are a criminal, you are sent to prison.

If you are a disobedient child, you are sent to your room.

The lore of someone being exiled has been around since the beginning of time and has carried through every step of storytelling.

As the cowboys would say, 'this town ain't big enough for the both of us.'

So, this results in a dual or confrontation where one party is exiled from either the town or in life.

This does not happen in sports. There is nothing in contracts that an athlete must leave if they lose.

However, it does happen in professional wrestling.

A "Loser Leaves Town Match" is a match stipulation where the loser... well, it's where the loser leaves town.

It is traditionally set up in result of two wrestlers hating each other so much that, like a cowboy, the promotion is not big enough for the both of them.

The behind-the-scenes workings of this are often for two reasons: contracts or retirement.

When a wrestler's stay at that wrestling company is over, one way to send them off is by booking them in a match like this.

Their contracted number of dates are up, and they are moving on to the next territory or endeavor.

This was much more common in the territory days where wrestlers would travel around like a band of gypsy carnival workers.

The older generations would keep their act fresh by hitting up new regions for an extended stay.

But this stay wouldn't be extended too far. Then it would be on to the next.

It is said that professional wrestlers are like the mafia because once you are in, you are always in.

But still, wrestlers DO retire.

This could be an opportunity to have a big send off with a big "Loser Leaves Town Match".

In some of these cases, it is not exactly the loser that will leave but rather one wrestler putting their career on the line.

This has resulted in favor of one putting their livelihood on the line, but in more memorable cases it would be the final chapter of a celebrated career.

The who is who of professional wrestling's legendary history has been involved in a "Loser Leaves Town Match" at some point.

Ric Flair would put his career on the line a few times. He would defeat Vader at Starrcade in 1993 so no careers were lost.

Ric Flair would lose to Shawn Michaels at WrestleMania 24. He would still go on to have matches in TNA Impact for a while.

WrestleMania 7 saw "Macho Man" Randy Savage end his career by losing to The Ultimate Warrior. He would be back about a year later.

Shawn Michaels would put his career on the line and lose to The Undertaker at WrestleMania 26.

The "Heart Break Kid" would stay true to his word until a random one-off match in Saudi Arabia.

Everyone comes back.

Whether it's preferred or not, they always come back.

However, Gorilla Monsoon would end his career by the hands of Ken Patera in a "Loser Leaves Town Match" way back in 1980.

A more recent example saw Mance Warner defeat MJF in a "Loser Leaves Match" but both performers would disappear in this situation.

There are a multitude of ways to settle a score.

When those days stop working, and the hatred and violence escalates to a boiling point, despite the fan's chants of 'fight forever', there must be a finale.

Nothing is forever.

Wrestlers leave and wrestlers return.

A "Loser Leaves Town Match" provides temporary closure, an exclamation point, on a bitter rivalry.

101 REASONS TO LOVE PRO WRESTLING

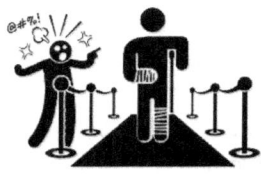

83. INJURY COMEBACKS

Everyone loves a good comeback.

Everyone can appreciate the pain and trauma of an injury.

We fall from our bikes before we can soar. But we get back up, we dust ourselves off, and keep going.

We love to see that person confined to a wheelchair or crutches take that first step back.

In sports, there are comebacks every week. However, the bigger comebacks get remembered.

The likes of Michael Jordan over his whole career, Reggie Miller scoring 8 points in 9 seconds against the New York Knicks in 1995, and many more have proved this true.

Injury comebacks are some of the most memorable comebacks.

This would be Tiger Woods returning to win a major.

Lance Armstrong beating cancer to have a successful return.

And Kerri Strug's gold medal performance at the 1996 Olympics.

Would the movie "Rocky" had been as enthralling if he had not been beaten up for a while before it?

An underdog coming back is always a sweet sight, but an underdog with a limp and multiple obstacles behind them is that much sweeter.

Professional wrestling is no stranger to this hypothetical sweetness.

Injury comebacks in professional wrestling happen for a few reasons outside of the obvious.

Yes, sometimes an injury comeback is because the wrestler is really injured and needs to tend to their ailment. This has given the fans some great moments.

Edge returning at the Royal Rumble after being absent for years due to a career ending injury.

The same could be said for Shawn Michaels, Daniel Bryan, and others who took an extended break from being an active wrestler due career ending injuries.

However, it could also be used to give someone some time off to recuperate from nagging pain or to give the wrestler to return with freshness.

John Cena returned after less than six months to the 2008 Royal Rumble to one of the biggest reactions of the pay per view history.

Shane McMahon comes and goes.

The same could be said for Brock Lesnar.

Chris Jericho has used time off to reinvent his character multiple times.

The Rock showing up is always possibility.

Even when it's promoted, the anticipation causes a stir among professional wrestling fans. It's truly a 'Beautiful Day'.

But when professional wrestling really wants to shock the crowd, the comeback is kept as a surprise.

When that music hits, and the returning superstar makes their way to the ring you never know what is going to happen next.

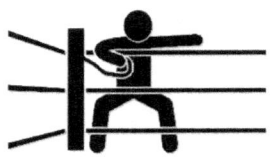

84. THE TAG ROPE

There are rules to everything.

Be it the law, school, work, or play, we all must abide by life's set of rules.

It's not just a commandment of how to live life.

It is also in every game we play.

If we pull the wrong card, we have no choice but to "Go to jail. Go Directly to jail. Do not pass go. Do not collect $200."

We must touch all four bases in order to get a Run when playing baseball.

When playing tag on the playground we are only safe at home base.

Like everything, professional wrestling has many rules but specifically pertaining to tags in tag team matches.

In the world of professional wrestling, tag team matches are a substantial segment of the variety of bouts that occur on nearly every card.

The big draws of history, the most historic feuds, and final match of the night is almost always the big one on one match-up.

These are the main events of most big events.

However, tag team wrestling is still very important if it's promoted that way.

It is said, and argued, that the first recorded tag team match was in 1901 in San Francisco.

Regardless of when, this match type definitely has it's long earned legacy.

This is where the rules and the tag ropes come to play.

In a traditional tag team match the rules are in place that one partner from each team must remain outside of the ring until they are tagged in.

Most would think, and in some cases that don't honor the rules, it would be as simple as tagging the partner and that is that.

However, there is a tag rope.

Another little component in the pageantry that is part of the show that is pro wrestling.

A rope that hangs from the top corner of the ring that wrestlers are to hold while being tagged.

This is in place to ensure the wrestler is not going too far to make the tag.

Otherwise, a wrestler could circle the ring and make tags as they please.

Essentially, it holds the tagged wrestler to be in their designated corner.

Good guys do it and bad guys don't.

Professional wrestling fans with a keen and knowing eye will notice that the tag ropes are often used on the back left and front right sides of the hard camera shot.

This is to allow the good guy team to showcase their emotion to the viewing crowd at home.

But more importantly, we, the viewer, gets to see the apron-standing face on the outside desperately reach in for the inevitable hot tag.

And hot tag it is... unless they are not holding the tag rope.

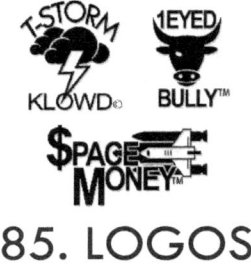

85. LOGOS

Symbols have been part of civilization since civilization has begun.

Ancient symbols were found in caves from times way before us.

These small artistic art pieces represent culture, clubs, societies, and in modern times, used as a branding logo.

Since the 1800's, thanks to the rise of the printing press, brands have been able to market themselves with mass produced physical materials.

Iconic logos have included Coca-Cola, McDonalds, Nike, Apple, and Starbucks, to name just a small few that have become embedded into our modern culture.

Rock bands and other musical artists would utilize logos to capture the vibe of the artist and give fans something to doodle on their notebooks in class.

In sports, the team logo is on the jerseys, displayed everywhere, and worn by the fans. This is how we identify the team and check the box scores.

A logo needs to be versatile, easy to recognize, unique, and something that can stand as a non-written depiction of personality.

It would be silly not to imagine professional wrestling adopting the same form of advertising and branding as every other company or artist.

In professional wrestling, image is everything.

Since its earliest days, the idea has been to sell tickets and make money. With this, comes promotional materials to do just that.

Wrestling companies would have logos and symbols to represent their business since the industry got off the ground.

The WWWF logo would evolve to the boxy and iconic WWF logo. Then this would evolve into the scratchy logo of the Attitude era. They'd "Get the F" out and then switch to the sharper lightening-like logo of the modern PG era.

Other companies would naturally have a logo to represent their product.

Professional wrestling is now praised for its spectacular production quality, but the design work throughout history goes unheralded.

Exact roots are easy to debate, but logos were around as long as something could be printed and sold in wrestling.

In the 1980's logos really took off as merchandising became a mainstream tactic.

There were many famous logos used for media, merchandise, and for production purposes.

The likes of Hulk Hogan's "Hulkamania", Roddy Piper's "Hot Rod", the Ultimate Warrior's make-up logo, Randy Savage's "Macho Man" text with sunglasses, and numerous more have been embedded into the minds of all longtime fans.

As time moved forward so did the graphic designs of some very memorable logos.

Sometimes the branding will catch on in a huge way like an nWo logo, the DX logo, Austin 3:16, Shawn Michaels' broken heart, Razor Ramon's razor blade, Bret Hart's winged skull, the Hardy Boyz symbol, Undertaker's X and T, CM Punk's fist and bolt, and all those iconic emblems.

Of course, we relate the logo to the performer. This makes a huge difference.

However, even the logos of those who did not catch on as big as those Hall of Fame performers are still memorable to many longtime fans.

A great logo does not automatically make the performer, but it sure as hell helps sell those t-shirts.

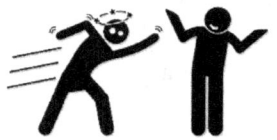

86. PUNCHING THE AIR IN DESPERATION

When all hope is lost, we do what we have to do.

Desperation is a form of panic that results in rash or extreme behavior.

In human nature, the most carnal display of this is fighting for survival.

It is an animalistic urge to keep going even though the odds are completely against you.

A horrendous example is the trapped rat that will gnaw their own limb off to escape.

It does not have to be that serious.

A losing sports team can also go for a 'Hail Mary' play in last ditch efforts to get the win.

It could as easily be someone doing whatever they can to get out of a situation they really want to get out of.

It could be a physical feat or doing something a little crazy to change one's circumstance.

There are numerous situations where hope is lost, or so we think, in the brutality that is professional wrestling.

There are many instances where a wrestler must resort to cheating to win.

This is often a bad guy tactic, however, sometimes a handful of tights or feet on the ropes are used to squeak out the victory.

101 REASONS TO LOVE PRO WRESTLING

Eddie Guerrero would "Lie, Cheat, and Steal" with a smile on his and the crowd's face.

Ric Flair was dubbed "The Dirtiest Player in the Game" for a reason.

But some acts of physical panic are the result of getting beaten down.

After a long grueling fight, there comes a time where a match can break down to a blow for blow fist fight.

Blows are traded between the fighters, and it is inevitable that one takes the best of it.

This often results in a dramatic point that is a sight to be seen.

One wrestler swings wildly, mentally and physically depleted, and punches the air in desperation.

They are all but knocked out on their feet, but their momentum carries on.

Lefts and rights are thrown to the wind before they are finally taken out.

This is the epitome of professional wrestling minutiae.

It's a small detail to compliment the big picture that is the match and show.

But it's also a feeling that anyone who has ever given their all, but came up short, can relate to.

It's said that it's always most honorable to go down swinging.

Sometimes that includes punching the air in desperation.

You never know what's going to connect.

You might as well close your eyes and just swing away.

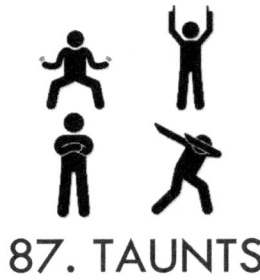

87. TAUNTS

When someone is successful, it is not unheard of for them to celebrate.

This happens, even on the field of competition.

In the heat of battle, one's celebration could also be a form of reactionary disrespect.

It is an insult in the form of a gesture.

The best example of this would be the end zone dances that football players would bust out in during a touchdown celebration.

However, the most simplistic would be that a good ol' middle finger being held up in the air.

If there is an open display of flaunting a celebration in the world of sports, it only pales in comparison to the taunts in professional wrestling.

The generic form of this, and likely the longest form of taunting in wrestling would have to be the oh so cliché muscle flex.

This would definitely evolve as wrestlers would create their own victory poses.

As things became more theatrical, taunts would begin to occur after not only when someone is victorious, but when a big move occurs or even just to antagonize the opponent.

Ric Flair's strut is known by most fans, but it was something done long before him.

John Cena would remind people that they cannot, in fact, see him.

Eddie Guerrero had his dance.

"Diamond" Dallas Page brought the "Diamond" hand gesture long before Jay-Z.

Randy Orton just raises his arms. Big Show raises just one.

Cactus Jack would "Bang-Bang".

The Hardy's throw up their fingers. Rob Van Dam only has to use his thumbs.

Shinsuke Nakamura busts out his "C'mon" pose.

The Rock has many up his elbow pad and is never shy to challenge others to "Bring It".

Booker T would celebrate with a Spinnaroni.

Every successful and unsuccessful performer has their signature poses, but some gestures are not as family friendly.

The middle finger is as part of "Stone Cold" Steve Austin's legacy as any character trait. The D-Generation X "crotch chop" is not something a child should be doing. Rick Rude would swivel his hips.

There are numerous more that have made their way into the pro wrestling ethos.

These gestures are not only done by those in the ring.

It is something you'll see in any crowd of excited fans.

This is just another way for a fan to show their love for their favorites and connect with the community of fans who feel the same.

In wrestling, that connection is everything... even if it does make us look pretty silly.

101 REASONS TO LOVE PRO WRESTLING

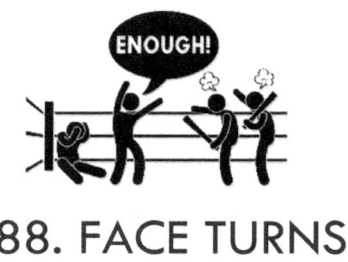

88. FACE TURNS

We are taught there is good and bad people at a young age.

There are saints and sinners.

We are to aspire for sainthood by bringing kindness and good to the world.

We are to reject sin, show discipline, and not exploit in our favor and show disregard for others.

No one's moral compass is written in stone. Things can change, people can evolve, and intentions can morph.

This is a story that has been told in all mediums.

A character sees the proverbial "light" and undergoes a transformation.

There have been numerous change-of-heart stories to both entertain and enlighten.

Charles Dickens' "A Christmas Carol" tells a tale of Ebenezer Scrooge going from a miserable old man to a changed man with a big heart.

The 1993 comedy classic "Groundhog Day" sees an egotistical jerk of a man redeem himself at the end of the story as someone who learned to appreciate life and the important of good deeds.

In professional wrestling there are these same moments of redemption.

A bad guy has a turning point in their character arc where they no longer portray evil.

It could be a split moment decision of right and wrong, where doing good is the chosen path.

In wrestling this happens to keep characters fresh, to tell a new story, or to ignite a huge reaction.

If a wrestler has been a bad guy for an extended period of time, the reaction starts to fade, and their impact on the show has lessened than a change is written in.

There are other situations where the wrestler has done all they can as a heel, and to level-up, and advance towards the main event, their character must grow.

That does not take away from the story being told.

From the fan perspective, it's a shock and surprise.

We have been conditioned to hate a character and then like a flip of a switch, we are given a reason to cheer them on in their new journey.

Many wrestlers will start off with one allegiance and move on to other and then back and forth. It is a useful device to keep a great career going.

The Undertaker would start off as a bad guy, but this would shift once he rejected the sadistic Jake "The Snake" Roberts in the early 1990's.

These are welcomed surprises and has been part of what has kept the story lines of professional wrestling prospering.

To list all face turns in professional wrestling would be to tell the tale of a hundred years of detailed stories but there are a few from the WrestleMania era of note.

At WrestleMania VII, Randy Savage lost a career versus career match against the Ultimate Warrior. This would be the moment that he would be able to change to a good guy.

WrestleMania would see multiple big moments like this.

In anticipation of WrestleMania 21, Batista quit the heel faction Evolution in favor of standing up for both himself and what was right.

WrestleMania 13 featured one of the best matches and biggest moments in wrestling. Bret "The Hitman" Hart entered as the good guy while the emerging "Stone Cold" Steve Austin entered as heel. By the end of the amazing story these two told, the roles were reversed.

It has also happened after other grueling matches. In 1989, at NWA's Clash of the Champions IX, Terry Funk shook Ric Flair's hand after losing a classic "I Quit" match.

Everyone is entitled to a change of heart and in professional wrestling hearts change all the time.

On a 1997 episode of Monday Night Raw, Vince McMahon stood in front of a camera and proclaimed that we longer live in a world that is black and white and that reality is shades of grey.

Good guys could have edge, bad guys could have positive attributes, and there would be no absolutes.

This is more aligned with the reality of human nature.

Professional wrestling is not the real world. The reality is a beast of its own.

In the great escape that is wrestling, we need the protagonists just as much as the antagonists to tell a great story.

Even if that means, the roles shift from time to time.

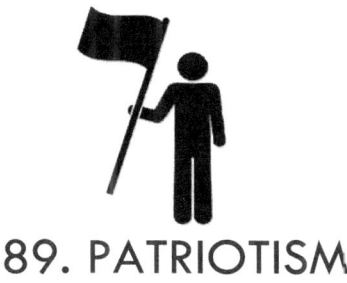

89. PATRIOTISM

Having a sense of pride in your domain is something instilled in our very being.

We wake up each day there and lay our heads to sleep in the same place.

It's home. It's where we experience life.

Holding a sentiment for the land that we represent is part of our culture on many levels.

Everyone has established roots somewhere.

We represent our domestic domicile, our cities, our states, and our countries.

Pride in one's country is patriotism.

Flags are waved, anthems are sung, pledges are made, and traditions are established.

There have always been stories in the history of existence of war and dispute.

Nothing is perfect and perfectly legitimate grievances could be had with one's homeland.

But these cultures continue to carry on. Children are raised, lives are lived, and these countries continue on with the culture. Even in that most genuine thought, it is hard to not have some sense of patriotism.

Professional wrestling is a collective of cultures so is a perfect vessel for the display of patriotism.

101 REASONS TO LOVE PRO WRESTLING

The early days of wrestling always had a showcase of country pride.

This would just be someone wrestling and representing their homeland.

Around World War 2, wrestling would mirror what has happening in the real world and introduced the trope of "evil foreign wrestler".

These performers, sometimes not actually from the country they claim, would display sad stereotypes of foreign lands.

Hawaiian born Tojo Yamamoto wrestled as an evil Japanese wrestler in the 1960's and 70's. He would travel the southern states of America and utilize the Pearl Harbor bombing to rile up the crowds.

Ivan Koloff, a Canadian playing a Russian, used the Cold War as his heat seeking catalyst.

There would be The Iron Sheik, Nikolai Volkoff, Colonel DeBeers, Haku, Kamala, and the great Yokozuna.

Then these anti-American wrestlers would battle it out with wrestlers who were portrayed as over the top pro-American heroes.

Seeing a wrestler come to the ring with an American flag was an easy way to pander to home-country fans.

Hulk Hogan was a flag waving hero that would take on all evil doers, including the foreign heels.

But even outside of him it would be hard not to put patriotic characters "Hacksaw" Jim Dugan and Sergeant Slaughter on the same level as jingoistic American fodder.

Others like Del Wilkes' "Patriot" character, Lex Luger, and Olympic gold medalist Kurt Angle have been a few of many more who have used American pride to rally the American fans.

These characters are completely outdated.

Thankfully, this trope did begin to evolve.

There are many wrestlers who are from different cultures, but they are not always defined as a bad guy just because they are from a different country.

There are still bad guys from every culture, but it's no longer mandatory.

Bret "The Hitman" Hart would be a proud Canadian wrestler, but the majority of his televised career saw him as one of the most beloved wrestlers of a generation.

There are plenty of international talent who are proud of where they come from, but also appreciated for the person they are and the morals they stand for.

There are still those who tout their American pride, as both good and bad characters.

Times need to continue change, but the landscape of wrestling is full of representation.

As new paths continue to be paved, patriotism is way to represent and open new doors.

Great wrestlers connect with the crowd no matter what flag they wave because great wrestling will always be without borders.

101 REASONS TO LOVE PRO WRESTLING

90. POST-MATCH RESPECT

Respect is a human quality that should exist regardless of anything.

Respect is a positive feeling or action that is shown to someone as a high regard.

In many cultures, this is an esteem that is earned.

Some cultures bow, smile, tip a hat, or they show respect in the form of a handshake.

In competition, respect is shown between competitors once the competition is over.

Professional wrestling is chaotic in its core, but those who participate and those who are fans definitely have an ethic of respect.

Everyone respects the business.

Like in any industry or community, the most talented and those who have put their time in typically get the most respect.

Committed fans, and obviously the wrestlers, respect everything that makes wrestling wrestling.

At the core of appreciation, fans should always respect their fellow human who puts their body on the line to provide this amazing form of escapism.

There is also a high level of respect between the wrestlers.

The core of this relationship is a trust between two humans collaborating on telling a very dangerous and physical story.

But the presentation of wrestling is built on good guys, bad guys, characters, and extreme competition.

There have been many moments that two wrestlers take a moment after a war to share in post-match respect.

The idea of wrestling is beating someone up with crazy moves.

Putting aside differences to recognize each other's skills, heart, passion, or for a great match was not always a common sight.

These moments were not used very often or without a genuine great performance was shared.

As wrestling has progressed, sportsmanship is no longer a surprising taboo.

Akin to amateur wrestling, Ring of Honor installed a "Code of Honor" into their matches where the competitors had to shake hands before the match.

Even outside of regulated devices like this, seeing two wrestlers shake hands after a hard fought and grueling fight is a common showcase of post-match respect.

These occasions are special.

It is like the show pauses for just a moment so two humans can share in a mutual appreciation.

And to be able to see this is thing of beauty.

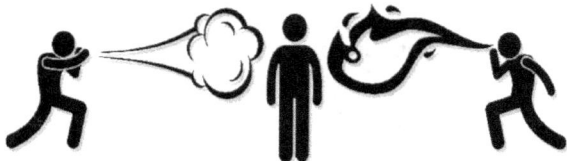

91. MISTING, POWDER, AND FIRE!

There will always be someone who has a moral compass that does not align with the rest of us.

We know of many examples of someone being caught, but for every person caught cheating there is an uncomfortable amount of those who aren't when you take a moment to ponder.

They seek a mischievous way to have the upper hand.

And this happens in all facets of life.

It occurs in business, in video games, and sports.

It's not ethical, moral, or fair... but it happens.

You just keep playing the game. You work hard. You overcome ALL obstacles.

You do what you have to do to survive, even if it is an underhanded surprise.

One common way to surprise an opponent in a schoolyard fight is grabbing a handful of dirt and throwing at your foe's unexpected eyes.

If there is a way to depict a good fight, then it is only natural that pro wrestling would put their spin on it.

In wrestling, there typically isn't dirt at ringside to use to one's advantage but there are a few devices that have found their way into the annals of the art.

Throwing an illegal object at someone's eyes is just one of many ways a heel will cheat to win or take out their enemy.

Normally these devices come in three popular forms.

A misting of some type of poisonous liquid. Throwing powder. Or, in some vicious cases... throw fire.

All to the eyes.

There are many people to use these contraptions in their matches, but only few who have absorbed these tactics as part of their legacy.

Inspired by an artistic theatre style of the same name, The Great Kabuki, was a mysterious Asian character that is credited as the first to use the idea of spitting mist at their opponent.

The Great Muta and Tajiri carried this tradition on with class and awe.

Still, others like Gangrel, Luna Vachon, and even Hornswoggle have put their spin on the attack.

It is not often applied, but there is even a lore about what each color means.

For instance, the classic green is used to merely obstruct vision but black will blind someone for weeks, blue will put someone to sleep, and so on.

However, powder to the eyes is also associated with another Hall of Famer in Yokozuna. When Yoko was in jeopardy, we would be aided by his evil manager Mr. Fuji, who would launch ceremonial salt into the opponent's eyes.

Fuji would use this cheat with other people he managed as even as a wrestler himself in the 70's.

This attack goes back a while in the timeline of wrestling. Masa Saito would use this heel tactic to become of the most hated wrestlers of his time.

Jerry "The King" Lawler and many others to toss salt or powder to take over the upper hand in a fight.

Fire is one of the most dangerous elements in play. In rare and crazy moments, someone will throw fire into the face of their adversary.

101 REASONS TO LOVE PRO WRESTLING

There have been a few notable "fireball to the face" moments.

One of our most primal lessons is that fire is in fact hot.

So, when wrestling fans see it used as an attack on someone's face it definitely stands out.

There have been real examples of this not going as planned, but this troupe is simple.

The wrestler uses flash paper and a lighter. The flash paper burns up in, not surprisingly, a flash.

When it is done correctly, the illusion tells the story of extreme pain.

Some wrestlers will attack their enemy with a chair, or a ladder, or a cane, or by throwing them through a table.

It takes a special breed of monster to go for the eyes.

If one cannot see, it makes it rather difficult to defend themselves.

The victims are then left to fend off an attack from any direction the attacker chooses.

It's unfair. It's cheap. It's downright heinous.

It's also a visual you never forget.

Whatever your poison, it is always a next day talking point when someone is blasted in the eyes with mist, powder, and fire!

92. ROYALTY

Hail to the king.

The concept of royalty is known by all.

It's the folks at the top of the food chain, the rulers, and the celebrated.

Originating with the feudal systems of medieval Europe, it has always been about power.

It's those who have the power due to owning land, having the most riches, and through a long line of nepotism.

This would carry on all the way into modern times.

The idea of a King or Queen is also gimmick that is used in marketing.

Michael Jackson was the "King of Pop".

American jazz performer Benny Goodman was the "King of Swing".

And of course, Lions have been given the title as "King of the Jungle".

It is status. It is a special acclaim. It is being the top of a hierarchy.

In professional wrestling, the performed hierarchy definitely has its share of royalty.

There have been many a men and women to wear a crown and lay claim to being king or queen.

Some wrestlers earn their moniker.

The WWE's King of the Ring tournament has gone from an annual Pay Per View to a random attraction in recent years.

This has both made and rejuvenated careers.

Owen Hart used his victory to proclaim himself as "The King of Harts".

The jealousy over the thrown was the reason Edge and Christian's long running tag team broke up.

The rap-friendly Mabel would become "King Mabel" and find himself in a bigger role on the card.

There are those like Baron Corbin who won and rode the character out without much career advancement.

Then there are the likes of Booker T, who take the crown and totally fade into an awesome character of royalty.

Others just pretty much call themselves "The King".

Jerry "The King" Lawler was not the only king in wrestling history.

The likes of King Curtis Iaukea, Jackie Fargo, King Haku, the "Macho King" Randy Savage, "King of the Mountain" Jeff Jarrett, and numerous other Barons, Dukes, and Princes.

This is essentially just another type of gimmick or character in the toy box of professional wrestling.

Some wrestlers wear silly costumes. Some of those include a royal attire.

Still, it becomes a status that the owner does not want to lose. They work hard to maintain their royalty, earned, or just given.

It could easily be said, heavy is the head that wears the crown.

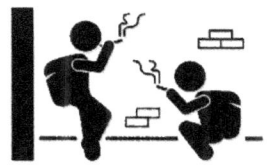

93. REBELLION

It is a natural urge to disobey authority.

We do not like listening to mean parents, mean teachers, and mean bosses.

Even if they do know better, we don't want to listen because we are the ones that really know better.

As we grow up these are either lessons learned or moments to be proud of. Maybe both.

There are still the bad apples that spoil the bunch. They rebel by breaking the law and hurting people.

Most folks walk the fine line and blend into the system, but some just like sticking it to the man.

These are the problem-makers, the disrupters, the rebels.

In movies and television, shows that feature the anti-hero are long part of its celebrated history.

We laughed at and with Archie Bunker, Al Bundy, and George Jefferson.

We were enthralled by the story line and characters like Walter White from "Breaking Bad" or Omar from "The Wire".

The world of professional wrestling is full of anti-heroes who have not been shied to showcase rebellion.

Professional wrestling's storytelling foundation is built on good guys versus bad guys.

101 REASONS TO LOVE PRO WRESTLING

Fans cheer the good guys on as they live out the fantasy of defeating the evil bad guys.

Sometimes this recipe does not meet the tastes of the audience.

The fans of wrestling will find a reason to cheer on the heel.

These larger-than-life anti-heroes rebel against the norm and the authority of wrestling.

It could be a simple attack on the referee, but there are many examples of great rebellion.

"Stone Cold" Steve Austin would rebel against Vince McMahon.

D-Generation X would also rebel against Vince.

The nWo rebelled against WCW.

It goes on and on.

If there is authority, there is someone rebelling against it.

In wrestling the authority represents the jerky boss, the stern teacher, and everything a normal person would dislike.

In the real world we swallow our pride and keep going because we need our grades, we need our jobs, and we depend on the system the authority figure is in charge of.

"Stone Cold" didn't swallow his pride. He got the best of his boss every week for our amusement.

D-Generation X and the New World Order definitely didn't either.

They took a more sophomoric approach, but it was rebellion all the same.

Everyone likes a bad boy.

101 REASONS TO LOVE PRO WRESTLING

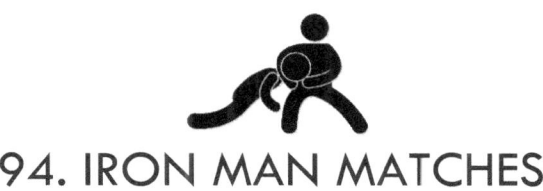

94. IRON MAN MATCHES

Of course, all comic book fans and most of the population by now know of the superhero known as "Iron Man".

Created by Stan Lee in 1963, Tony Stark was born as new Marvel Comics icon.

One of Black Sabbath's, and all of rock music's, best song is indeed "Iron Man".

Recorded in 1970 and released in 1971, Ozzy Osbourne, Tony Iommi, Geezer Butler, and Bill Ward would unleash one of the catchiest and rawest heavy metal songs of all time.

There is Cal Ripken Jr., known as the "Iron Man" because his insanely long streak of never missing a Major League Baseball game.

Breaking Lou Gehrig's streak of 2,130 games seemed unbreakable until this Hall of Famer broke the streak and surpassed it with 2,632 consecutive games played.

The term "Iron Man" is often associated with the idea that someone has showcased a feat of endurance and defeats all odds.

Then they do it again and again maintaining the reputation of being someone who excels.

Professional wrestling has its fair share of tests of endurance.

The most common form of this is the classic "Iron Man Match".

Two or even more opponents face off for a set amount of time, often 30 or 60 minutes, and whoever has the most wins at the end is declared the victor.

Time is money. Commercials need to air, and promoters need to get on at least a decent amount of wrestlers on every card.

101 REASONS TO LOVE PRO WRESTLING

Thus, the "Iron Man Match" is reserved for oh so special occasions.

The origin of the "Iron Man Match" is debatable.

Wrestling matches going back to the carnival days were long and brutal.

Sometimes these bouts would be best out of three falls. Sometimes two performers would just go "Broadway".

"Going Broadway" is the backstage term for a match that goes for an hour, often with indecisive results.

But the "most wins in a certain time frame" construct of an "Iron Man Match" started off under the aptly named "Marathon Match".

The earliest on record were untelevised tag matches between The Rockers and The Fabulous Rougeau Brothers. These would go an hour with The Rockers winning the half dozen or so of these spread out during the WWF tour of 1989.

WCW would adopt the match idea as well. In 1992 and 1993, Rick Rude would compete in two of these matches against Ricky Steamboat and Dustin Rhodes respectively.

In 1993, Bret "The Hitman" Hart would win his first WWF World Title via an Iron Man Match against "Nature Boy" Ric Flair.

In 94, Bret Hart would defeat his brother Owen in a handful of house show matches that featured 60 Minute Iron Man bouts.

However, it would be WrestleMania 12 to put this match on the map.

Bret Hart would take on Shawn Michaels in a 60-minute Iron Match that main evented one of the biggest shows of all time.

It would take an "over time", but "The Heartbreak Kid" Shawn Michaels would realize his boyhood dream as he finally captured the beloved winged eagle version of the WWF World Title.

From there, every few years the illustrious "Iron Man Match" would pop back up when rivalries were heated enough.

Triple H and The Rock would square off in one at Judgement Day in 2000.

Brock Lesnar and Kurt Angle had one on free television at a Smackdown in 2003.

Kurt Angle and Shawn Michaels ran a thirty-minute Iron Man on RAW in 2005.

John Cena and Randy Orton had one at Bragging Rights in 2009.

The most notable of recent Iron Man matches was in NXT as Bayley defeated Sasha Banks at NXT Takeover: Respect. It was only a 30-minute match but is heralded as one of the best female matches in WWE history.

Rightfully so, it was amazing.

Many of these mentioned Iron Man matches and many others were also amazing.

These matches aren't exclusive to WWE.

Tony Deppen and Jordan Oliver had a great Iron Man Match at a GCW event in early 2021. This Iron Man Match went two hours.

Deppen would also take on Trish Adora in 2021 for an Intergender Iron Match presented by Pro Wrestling Illustrated.

While it's not as common as ladder or cage match, these bouts still happen.

When they do, it's best to just sit back and enjoy the ride.

To be a professional wrestler, one must be ready for anything and endure physical hell all for the love of wrestling.

But an "Iron Man Match" is a totally different level of endurance.

You have to be ready to go the distance.

101 REASONS TO LOVE PRO WRESTLING

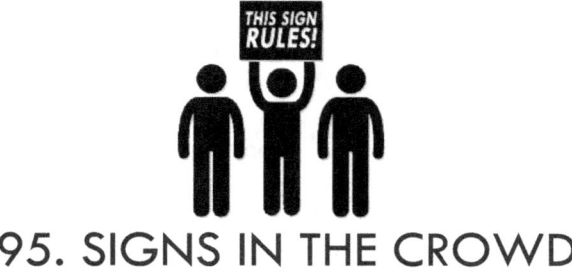

95. SIGNS IN THE CROWD

When people gather some want to stand out and be noticed.

When rapid sports fans go to games, they wave flags, towels, and other items in support of their team.

Some even bring signs.

Political rallies see crowds of party line supporters get loud and cheer on their selective candidates.

They bring their signs as well.

Protests over causes see crowds of like-minded people gathering to make their voice heard.

They have signs too.

People like getting and giving attention and those people include professional wrestling fans.

Wrestling fans have followed the trends of everyone else that gathers crowds and have brought homemade signs to the show.

In the earliest days, it was simple and fun. Kayfabe was well alive with signs rooting on the good guys and jeering the jerks on the show.

We would see fans hold up signs for "Hulkamania" and other 80's icons.

The signs were as innocent as the times.

As time went on, pop culture changed. It got edgier and a lot snarkier.

Signs got a bit raunchier.

They got a little off topic.

Then they started promoting themselves.

They got a bit ruder and more offensive.

The signs encompassed insider terms and complained about the shows on more behind the scenes level.

In more recent years, they've started on-going debates like about video game preference.

Some would say the best signs are the ones that go a few seats into a row of fans that all collaborate to deliver a message.

Whatever the message is, a sign in the crowd is part of the show.

This is part of the bond that a fan has with the product.

Someone was so excited about going to the show that they pulled out some poster board, markers, and put their perspective out there for the world to see.

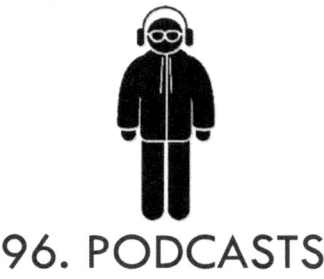

96. PODCASTS

Everyone has things they're interested in.

It could be a hobby to occupy our time, a cultural ritual, or just an escape from reality.

With that, the fans of these things absorb as much as they can about it.

Comic book fans, sports nuts, and religious folks all have their lineages, statistics, lore, and behind the scenes news.

In older times, word of mouth and then books would be our source of information.

Then radio and television opened doors to sensory overload.

The next logical step in the progress of information has been podcasts.

At first an audio medium and then video.

Professional wrestling fandom is as fanatical as any comic book, sport, or religious following and the fans want to know everything.

Before podcasts, the insider information that wrestling fans craved came from magazines that were out of date by the time they hit newsstands, overrated newsletters written by so-called experts, and then low-quality shoot interviews that would be swapped by VHS collectors.

Podcasts in wrestling would change this.

Information from behind the curtain would be available weekly and even daily by fans, reporters, and the wrestlers themselves.

Colt "Boom Boom" Cabana's "The Art of Wrestling" was one of the first of these recorded shows in 2010.

Getting the perspective of a respected wrestler, sharing their experiences, and speaking to others was groundbreaking at the time.

Numerous other wrestlers from the past and present have their own shows now.

Some even group together under network umbrellas. Bruce Pritchard, Jeff Jarrett, Eric Bischoff, and others all release weekly shows for Conrad Thompson's adfree shows network.

Vince Russo has his own thing, as does numerous others.

Even the WWE has delved into the world of podcast style interview shows.

The very people responsible for the memories and moments in the ring, from backstage, or even running the show now share stories from the past, clear up lies, and present their personal perspective on events occurred.

It's also the current events too. Every pro wrestling news site also has podcasts in both audio and video form.

Every show has dozens of reviews and recap shows by media, and fans alike, moments after ending.

Interviews with wrestlers are dropped every day without fans having to wait on a fourth generation copy of a VHS shoot tape.

If something big happens, it is only a matter of minutes before someone is on YouTube sharing the news and their take on the situation.

Technology has evolved, but a professional wrestling fan's desire for information, content, and detail is something they'll always subscribe to.

101 REASONS TO LOVE PRO WRESTLING

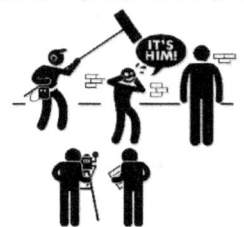

97. POP CULTURE POP-UPS

Pop culture is a wild scope and combination of the arts, trends, and flavors of the month.

Since the beginning of television, famous people who were not actors would pop-up.

Iconic baseball players and other sport stars would be heralded with the same acclaim and fame as anyone else at the top of people's collective minds.

This goes from Los Angeles Dodger pitcher Don Drysdale showing up on "Leave it to Beaver" to Monkees singer Davy Jones popping up on "The Brady Bunch".

Stevie Wonder could be seen on "The Cosby Show".

Muhammad Ali made an appearance on "Diff'rent Strokes"

Sammy Davis Jr. made history on "All in the Family".

Since it's incarnation, hundreds of well-known celebrities have lent their voice to the Simpsons.

First Lady Michelle Obama even popped up on an episode of "iCarly".

There are numerous examples of these type of appearances.

It's fun for the fans of these folks to see them on other shows.

The cross-contamination of celebrity, of the arts, and of entertainment is a great way to achieve synergy between everything that is pop culture.

101 REASONS TO LOVE PRO WRESTLING

Some doors are harder to open and definitely rarer to see occur.

Professional wrestling is many things and niche is one of them, so it is always exciting for fans when there are pop culture pop-ups.

Despite the millions of fans, prime time television placement, and amazing talent of the performers the world of wrestling is often on the outskirts of mainstream entertainment.

Some performers bring crossover appeal by coming to wrestling from other fields.

Since wrestling's earliest days, other athletes have had notable careers.

Other outsiders have dipped their toes in for big events or to participate in a story line.

In rare cases, this is reversed.

"The Rock" Dwayne Johnson is one of the biggest Hollywood stars of all time.

Dave Bautista has been in some of the biggest movies of recent times.

John Cena has and is making his own imprint in film as well.

In the 1980's, Hulk Hogan was so popular that he starred in a handful of not-so-popular, but pretty memorable movies.

Chris Jericho has hosted things, popped up in movies, and is a singer in a rock band.

There are multiple examples of this kind of occurrence.

But these cross overs are rarely in the form of wrestling.

Seeing professional wrestling presented in other forms of media is a rare treat for fans.

It's a cycle.

101 REASONS TO LOVE PRO WRESTLING

Sometimes wrestling is a bigger thing in the eyes of pop culture and sometimes it's a side show people snicker at.

When it's hot, a wrestler shows up in something totally unrelated to wrestling that it's bizarre.

Sometimes the productions are treating wrestling as a novelty, but it is a novelty that brings in viewers.

Arsenio Hall would bring on professional wrestlers in character and talk to them like he would a normal guest.

There has been a plethora of sitcoms over the years to have an episode about professional wrestling. With this, comes a guest appearance or two and plenty of hijinks.

Hogan would show up everywhere.

"Macho Man" Randy Savage was the spokesman for Slim Jim jerky for years.

The biggest honor to most television nerds would go to Bret "The Hitman" Hart, who appeared on an episode of The Simpsons.

A bunch of WCW wrestlers appeared on Baywatch during the show's peak run.

In the 90's, the Attitude era made it really easy to be an "open fan" of wrestling.

A slew of wrestlers would show up and participate in Fear Factor, a gross-out television show hosted by Joe Rogan that was popular in the early 2000's.

Wrestlers have also appeared on Family Feud in a few different eras and would also be on an episode of the Weakest Link.

Triple H would appear on The Drew Carey Show.

Lita was on Dark Angel.

"Stone Cold" Steve Austin was on Nash Bridges.

The Rock would even host Saturday Night Live before taking over Hollywood to help promote WrestleMania 2000.

John Cena showed up on Hannah Montana.

A fan of professional wrestling getting to see Vader on "Boy Meets World" was just all kinds of awesome.

Professional wrestling is its own contained world so when that world spills into other things it gives the outside world a glimpse of "our" world.

It's just a little moment where you feel like wrestling is being accepted and it's okay to be a fan.

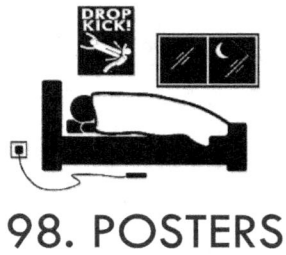

98. POSTERS

Communication and expression come in multiple forms.

Audible expression comes in the form of speech, singing, and screams.

Visual comes via artwork, printed text, video, and other mediums.

One medium is posters.

With Lithography's late 1700's roots, this platform has had many years to develop.

The first of these posters were called "broadsides" and featured marketing promotions and public announcements.

A successful and purposeful poster is two things: informative and eye-catching.

In the late 1800's, Toulouse-Lautrec's "Moulin Rouge" poster proved that it could be these two things, but also beautiful art.

Posters would eventually be used for multiple reasons including advertising a film, an album, or an event.

These would become collectible and treated like fine art because people would want to display them with pride.

The demand and production process would both evolve.

It wouldn't be long before people would have posters of their favorite cartoon characters, sports heroes, rock bands, and more covering their walls.

101 REASONS TO LOVE PRO WRESTLING

There would be no reason that professional wrestling would not want their place on the walls of their fans.

The earliest wrestling posters were beautiful event posters.

These were informative pieces that let viewer see when the show was, where it was being held, ticket prices, and touted the big matches intended to draw the interest of the fans.

This would grow into full on cinematic looking posters to promote a pay per view.

Pro wrestling posters do not end with events.

Like someone displaying their favorite sports stars, fans of wrestling also showcase their favorites.

Some even take this one step further and get their posters signed making them highly sought-after collectibles.

It could be as simple as a great photographer snapping the perfect shot to blow up into poster form.

It could be a promo shot with some additional graphic design.

It could be a collage of wrestlers or photos.

It could even be fine-art quality prints.

Regardless of what the visual is, if wrestling fans would want it and have no issue paying their hard-earned cash for it you can rest assured that it is being printed as we speak.

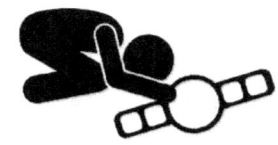

99. SACRIFICE

It is where passion and perseverance meet and then take the strenuous steps towards reaching one's goal.

Sacrifice is not a fly by night donation of time, effort, or funds.

It's difficult. It's tough. It's something one MUST do for whatever their reasons are.

Soldiers sacrifice their time, and sadly sometimes their lives, to defend their countries.

Every day parents sacrifice for the better of their children.

A business owner will do whatever they have to do to make sure their business succeeds or even stays afloat.

Athletes will play through injuries in their pursuit of reaching their goals.

If one has passion for anything, it's not surprising that we push our limits to do what we feel is needed.

Professional wrestlers are no stranger to sacrifice.

The physicality of professional wrestling is nothing to joke about.

These performers are taking a large toll on their bodies every single bump they take.

This leads to injuries they work through when they can regardless of what it does to their long-term health.

This leads to being forced to get multiple surgeries in order to be able to do what they love.

This leads to addiction to pain killer medication to mask the pain.

101 REASONS TO LOVE PRO WRESTLING

The wrestlers who love what they do, want to achieve, and need to support their families keep going.

Like a touring rock star, wrestlers spend a large chunk of their life on the road away from family and home.

Ultimately, children grow up without their parents.

Sadly, due to all of these factors the lives of some our favorite performers are cut short.

Their legacies live on forever.

We can turn on old matches or share memories with fellow fans.

For those outside of the professional wrestling bubble it would be hard to imagine this kind of sacrifice being had over something like a professional wrestling performance.

Pro wrestling is often a blip on the radar to most people, but to those that love the art form, it can be everything.

Some performers might not be our favorites, but that respect should always be there.

Chasing the glory of their best days, constantly reaching for the brass ring, and going through hell and back to entertain us fans should never be taken for granted.

101 REASONS TO LOVE PRO WRESTLING

100. COMEDY

Comedy is defined as a genre that consists of humorous discourse.

The goal is amusement and laughter.

It's in literature, theatre, and other types of performance art.

For every satire piece in books, there's a Weird Al doing comedic music.

For every stuffy politician using a joke to break the ice, there are iconic stand-up comedians who have made arenas erupt in laughter.

It's been said that comedy pushes the line of tragedy. If it bends, it's funny. If it breaks, it's tragic.

If someone trips and falls in a comedic manner it can be hilarious.

If they get badly hurt, it's not so hilarious.

Life deals us many ups and downs.

Some of it is just funny.

The giggle of a baby is music to the ears, but a baby crying is unsettling.

Someone being overly confident and failing is fun for those watching the ego trip take a bad turn.

Comedy is more than a genre of storytelling. It's life.

Professional wrestling encompasses all aspects of life in one way or another. Comedy is definitely an element that has its place.

101 REASONS TO LOVE PRO WRESTLING

There are a wide variety of different personas in wrestling that are all trying to stand out and be remembered by the viewers.

One character type that has had stellar results is the comedy wrestler.

These silly gimmicks bring a smile to the faces of the crowd and have had success on different levels over the different eras of wrestling.

Gorgeous George was so obscure that people had no choice but to laugh.

Andy Kaufman's crazy interactions with Jerry Lawler and Memphis was hilarious.

It goes on and on.

It could be pushing the taboos of sex like a Goldust, Val Venis, or "Sexual Chocolate" Mark Henry.

Others like Santino Marella, R-Truth, Hurricane Helms, and more just bring silly cartoon-like tropes to become and remain beloved by the audience.

Manager-slash-commentator legend Bobby "The Brain" Henan was always a hated heel, but it was hard not to laugh at the many great one-liners he had.

It's not just the characters.

Some cut sarcastic or humorous promos to amuse the crowds, but their in-ring work is nothing to laugh about.

These are your Rocks, New Days, Edge and Christians, Chris Jerichos, Booker Ts, and D-Generation X's.

There are also moments to make viewers cackle.

Mick Foley pulling a sock puppet from his pants to assist in his matches.

"Stone Cold" Steve Austin's interactions with Vince McMahon.

This is a case of the bad guy getting his comeuppance and there are a lot more examples of this.

Like McMahon, The Miz, Ric Flair, and other over the top egos have rightfully seen themselves the butt of many jokes.

The miscues and mistakes also bring the joy.

As was the debut of The Shockmaster. He was supposed to come through a wall like the Kool-Aid man, but fell down in the process.

Scott Steiner and Sid Vicious has unintentionally made people laugh with poorly thought-out promos.

When it's well done, it works.

When it's genuinely funny, it works.

Yes, professional wrestling is a brutal display of athletic competition.

It's not always going to be a laugh riot, but to deny comedy's place in wrestling would be, well, laughable.

101. ANYTHING... CAN... HAPPEN

We experience many things during our time here on Earth, but most days are spent in the mundane everyday nonsense.

We go to school. We go to work. We come home. We sleep. We interact with family and friends. We rinse and repeat.

David Byrne said it best, "How did I get here?"

Thankfully, this is broken up with hobbies, passions, and distractions.

Thankfully, we choose our own reality.

We get lost in religion, sports, or other forms of ritual.

It's how we wind down from the trials and tribulations of life.

And the best shocks to the system are when something out of the ordinary happens.

This spontaneous magic could be our favorite sports team getting the big win, getting excited for a new movie release, or even just finding an abandoned dollar bill on the sidewalk.

That's the beauty of life.

Excitement and escape can come from anywhere and it can happen at any time.

This happens every day in professional wrestling.

At its core, professional wrestling is a lot of different things to a lot of different people.

Wrestling is Santa Claus, a chance to live in a child-like gaze.

101 REASONS TO LOVE PRO WRESTLING

Wrestling is a riddle, something to constantly trying to figure out.

Wrestling is art. The performances are awe-inspiring feats with a beautiful story told in the ring.

Wrestling is an escape, a chance to disconnect from our day-to-day lives and just indulge.

Wrestling is a community. We have good family members and those we avoid.

Wrestling is life. Lived and breathed from generation to generation.

Wrestling is literally everything.

That's why when Vince McMahon would scream, "Anything can happen in the World Wrestling Federation" we, the fans of professional wrestling, believed him.

It was a slogan for the WWF in the 1990's, but it's true about all of professional wrestling... anything CAN happen.

Wrestling, when treated the way it should be, is a blank canvas ready to be covered with as much obscurity as possible.

Crazy surprise wins can easily happen on any given night.

Surprise appearances can lift you to your feet in excitement.

The top of pop culture has shown up from Hollywood and the music industry.

And on the contrary, Muppets, Robocop, Chuckie the doll, and Zombies have made their presence felt.

Our heroes can finally achieve their goals and it means something because we've been there every step of the way.

We laugh, we cry, we cheer, we boo, and we experience all realms of emotion thanks to wrestling.

Ultimately, professional wrestling is a dream come true.

101 REASONS TO LOVE PRO WRESTLING

Year to year, month to month, and day to day we delve into the landscape of wrestling.

We could have a horrible day at school, work, or home but professional wrestling is always there.

We could have the best day of our lives and professional wrestling is there to share in the moments.

Wrestling is friendship, community, and love when it's not always there in the real world.

It's catching the wind of a superhero's cape.

It's overcoming struggles of someone we can relate to.

It's the feeling of someone else's shoes for an experience outside of our norm.

At its core, professional wrestling is a culture of hope.

We anticipate the results going the way we'd like them to go.

Sometimes this is simply a wrestler getting the World Title.

It could also be wanting to see the bad guy get his just deserves.

It may be wanting to see the best athletes square off in a match rated five stars by a fellow fan.

We're not always going to see our favorites win, but as the great David Lee Roth proclaimed, "It's not whether you win or lose, it's how you good you looked doing it."

That's why we buy tickets and tune in.

We, as a collective community, share in the anticipation.

Professional wrestling fans all choose our own reality.

The depth of a wrestling fans knowledge of the business is now a self-restrained perspective thanks to the internet.

101 REASONS TO LOVE PRO WRESTLING

We can be simple and pure wide-eyed innocent fans, cheering on our favorites and booing the ones we hate.

Or we can also dive deep and debate over television ratings and shout from the mountains about the promoter's decisions.

Of course, most of us are somewhere in between.

Regardless, we are a family of fans.

We speak our own language, and all have strong opinions of what has, is, and will be presented.

This is not a construct that is fit for everyone.

Some people just don't get it, and never will.

But when you do, it's genuinely a magnificent piece of one's life.

Essentially, when it's all said and done, a wrestling show is a room of people surrounding a square with three ropes to engage in the athletic theatrics as told by some of the best artists, performers, and athletes in the world.

This and everything in between, is part of the magic and it's always there exactly when you need it.

There are many, many reasons to love pro wrestling…

ABOUT THE AUTHOR

I have many reasons to love professional wrestling outside of these 101 chapters. I have been a fan my entire life. My first memory was watching WWF's "Saturday Nights Main Event" as a small child. The main memories are flashes of the general energy of the show. When I was five, with the help of a family friend, I was blessed with the opportunity to go backstage at a WCW show at the Omni in Atlanta, GA. This is where I really started to grasp that pro wrestling was not just fun to watch but a creative business. This lead to a unique pre-internet perspective about what wrestling was, is, and could be.

I saw wrestling as something more than "good versus bad". I saw it as a creative outlet for everyone involved. I'd not just play with the wrestling figures my parents and grandparents bought me. I'd "book" them into storylines, gave "pushes" to my favorites, and would write down the entire experience. This would lead to joining internet fantasy wrestling leagues that were ran through email. To say it was an obsession would be an understatement.

Eventually in high school, I'd meet up with misfits that were just obsessed with wrestling as me. While they wrestled in the backyard, I'd help craft characters, promos, and treated it like I was the promoter. We'd all hang out, go to local independent shows, and before I knew it my friends were getting legitimately trained to bump. Using the money I got from my high school graduation open house, we went to directly to pay the rent for a local community center so we could run our first independent event. We'd pass out flyers, tell everyone, and do all we could to fill up those seats. Sometimes we would and sometimes we wouldn't, but it gave us all an outlet to live a dream. I would make lifelong friends, meet interesting people, and really live a dream I never thought possible while growing up.

This would last a few years. A lot of us would move on to the next phases of our lives, a few would wrestle for years after, and even one would "make it" to the big show. Regardless, I consider these men and women, the Maniaks, my family for life.

I'd eventually get a college degree, start a career, buy a house, and get a family of my own, but those memories of seeing wrestling as a kid, playing with those toys, and running my own independent wrestling company will remain with me forever.

www.ingramcontent.com/pod-product-compliance
Lightning Source LLC
Chambersburg PA
CBHW070319220526
45465CB00013B/958